Spanish America
1900–1970

Spanish America

1900–1970

TRADITION AND
SOCIAL INNOVATION

Fredrick B. Pike

W.W. NORTON & COMPANY, INC.
New York

For Helene

Library of Congress Cataloging in Publication Data

Pike, Fredrick B.
  Spanish America, 1900–1970.

  (Library of world civilization series)
  Bibliography: p. 169
  1. Latin America—Social conditions.   2. Social
classes—Latin America.   I.   Title.
HN110.5.A8P48   1973   301.24'098   73-4903
ISBN 0-393-05488-8
ISBN 0-393-09340-9 (pbk.)

2 3 4 5 6 7 8 9 0

Printed and bound in America

Contents

Preface

Attempting to present only one of countless views and perspectives, this book deals with Spanish America principally from the beginning of this century to the 1960s. In a few instances the events covered reach into the early 1970s. To my mind the twentieth century begins in Spanish America at that point, falling only approximately around 1900 and varying widely from country to country, when social problems became so acute as to threaten the established order. From this moment, Spanish American leaders had to take the masses more seriously into account and attempt to pacify them, the alternative being to risk social revolution and the destruction of tradition. This development is what divides the twentieth century from the preceding one.

To avoid undue complexity and length, this book is limited to Spanish America, although Brazil, the Portuguese-speaking giant of the American hemisphere, conforms to many of the patterns that are outlined. Generally, the countries of Central America do too, as well as Ecuador and Paraguay, none of which is treated in this necessarily selective study. Furthermore, Spain, though seldom brought directly into the account, lurks almost constantly in the background. The *madre patria* of the Spanish-speaking republics of the New World not only conformed essentially to the models described, at least until the profound social and economic changes achieved during the Francisco Franco régime, but also, in its Castilian centre and Andalusian south, originated many of them, a fact that gives some unity to an otherwise wildly diverse Hispanic world.

For invaluable suggestions during the preparation of this book I am profoundly grateful to two graduate students then at Notre Dame, Gabriel Marcella and Anthony O'Brien. Insights provided by O'Brien lie behind many of my analyses. In addition I am indebted to two Notre Dame professors, Thomas J. Stritch and Michael Francis, who read and commented upon an early draft of my manuscript. Above all, the constant encouragement of my wife, Helene, made it possible to bring this study to completion. For its errors and shortcomings I alone am responsible.

South Bend/Indiana
Fredrick B. Pike

7

1 Diego Rivera's mural, *Slavery at the Mill* (1930), showing Indian workers harvesting the sugar crop, overseen by their European exploiters, symbolizes the historical division of Spanish American society as seen by a Marxist champion of the Indian cause. Rivera's work shows no perception of the paternalism that has been a vital ingredient in Spanish America's traditional society.

1 Turn-of-the-Century Spanish America: Traditional Society and a Revolutionary Challenge

The most noteworthy feature about generation after generation of Spanish American leaders has not been their inability to attain political stability. Rather, it has been their awesome success in achieving what they view as infinitely more important: social stability. This book examines the uncanny skill of the directing classes of Spanish America in preserving the traditional social order against the multiple forces of change.

By traditional society in Spanish America is meant a society divided into two components with life styles and values so dissimilar that they must be described as distinct cultures. At the top is a dominant culture, vastly complex in its composition and frequently split by internal divisions. Beneath it lies a vast lower mass or subordinate culture, generally, for the sake of brevity, referred to as a sub-culture. It too is made up of many elements. Some of these, domestic servants and unskilled urban manual labourers, for example, may be in intimate contact with the dominant culture. Others, among them unassimilated Indians, are isolated and remote from the dominant culture.

Perhaps the most salient feature distinguishing the sub-culture is its lack of a capitalist orientation. Its members are resigned to a subsistence existence and are not motivated by a success myth that leads them to expect a more affluent tomorrow as a result of competitive skills. They live in the present and find it difficult to conceive of a future that is better than or essentially different from the present. Relatively quarantined against the incentives of individualistic, capitalist materialism, moreover, men of the sub-culture tend to have a collectivist outlook. To many of them, collectivist labour and land-utilization patterns are apt to seem natural and congenial.

Another significant characteristic of the sub-culture, one closely associated with its non-capitalist orientation, is the willingness of its members to live in a state of dependence. Concerned with security rather than independence, they rely on the paternalism of those above to keep them from sinking beneath the level of subsistence. Whether this paternalism is extended by the Church, a private *patrón* (owner-management) group or the state is unimportant. All that matters is that privately or publicly the men and institutions of the dominant culture assume the responsibilities and burdens involved in being depended upon by those below.

9

2 Indian traders at a Bolivian market: though their Socialist admirers have suggested that Indians are immune to capitalist incentives, many other observers have argued that their life style is naturally capitalist.

Among isolated Indian groups in such countries as Mexico, Guatemala, Ecuador, Bolivia and Peru, dependence is often less pronounced than in the case of sub-culture groups living in more intimate contact with higher social sectors. Indians dwelling in remote *comunidades* (communities) are relatively self-sufficient, producing themselves the goods that maintain them in a subsistence existence, whether these are food products they consume themselves or commodities sold to a local market to provide cash for the purchase of a few essentials. For whatever cash income they receive, however, and for the few finished goods they require, these Indians are dependent upon the mechanisms of a local, regional or even national economy over which they have no control. This situation is accepted because any endeavour to transform the market place into a more benign agency would perforce entail increased contact with the outside, non-Indian world. Suspicious of and sometimes overtly hostile to that world, Indians tend to regard dependence on its economic mechanisms, even when these are manifestly harsh, as infinitely preferable to integration into it. Within their status of economic dependence, then, they opt for maximum cultural freedom. By avoiding integration, they maintain the freedom to live almost exclusively in the domain of their own language, social habits, dress and eating styles, beliefs, prejudices and myths. Decidedly missing from their world of cultural values is a faith in steady progress towards individual mastery of nature and control of destiny.

In stark contrast, members of the dominant culture live almost as much in the future as in the present. They are motivated by the belief that individual action taken in the present can render the future more comfortable and secure. In short, they employ the perspectives associated with capitalism. These perspectives persist regardless of how ambivalent, ambiguous and unorthodox their attitudes towards capitalism often are – attitudes that will be described in the course of this book. Appreciating the value of individual capital accumulation in ensuring independence and self-reliance and in providing for the future, men of the dominant culture are little inclined towards patterns of collective ownership.

During the first two or three generations after independence had been achieved in the second and third decades of the nineteenth century, Spanish America's two cultures coexisted with at least the outward appearance, and perhaps at most times the actual substance, of harmony. On the rare occasions when conflict – which critics of the traditional society maintain was endemic, albeit cunningly masked by subtle means of repression – became outwardly manifest, the directing classes resorted to overt suppression. By and large, however, they did not have to do so.

One reason for the infrequency of a total breakdown of peaceful social relations was that men of the dominant culture were on the whole content to leave those of the sub-culture alone; they did not intrude unduly into their world, interfere with them or question their life styles. As a result members of the sub-culture were permitted at least that sense of dignity that comes when there is little criticism of their way of life by the leaders of society. In addition, those at the top of society showed at least some willingness to accept the obligations of paternalism. The upper classes honoured their paternalistic obligations partly because, true to values that can be traced back at least as far as medieval Spain, they associated resignation and poverty with virtue rather than vice. In ministering to the needs of the masses, then, they were rewarding virtue, not indulging vice.

Attitudes among the dominant culture, inherited from the colonial past and continuing to prevail to some considerable extent even beyond the mid-twentieth century, help to explain the subtle manner in which racial discrimination has operated in Spanish America. The social structure has aptly been described as a 'pigmentocracy', and the darker-skinned masses at the bottom were not expected to rise socially and economically, except in the case of certain extremely unusual individuals. Because they were not expected to rise, but were regarded as most virtuous when they uncomplainingly kept the lowly place in society regarded as proper for them, they

3 Maximo Pacheco's *The Noon Meal*, one of the many murals expressing the dignity of the Indian way of life produced in the aftermath of the Mexican Revolution.

4 Poster celebrating the sixth anniversary of the Cuban revolution. Coming to power in 1959, Castro was the first (and in the early 1970s still the only) Spanish American leader to succeed, at least in the short run, in eradicating the traditional two-culture society.

were not dismissed as morally inferior when they failed to advance in social status and economic power. As a result a dark skin, generally associated with poverty, was not taken as a badge of vice, although it was as often as not associated with limited intellectual potential.

The situation changed when assertive liberal elements appeared among the dominant culture and began to intrude into the world of the sub-culture, hoping, in many instances, to reform and uplift that world. It was their contention that the masses below should be reformed by being pressured into acquiring the more individualistic, self-reliant, materialistic and capitalist orientation of bourgeois elements within the dominant culture.

In so far as they grew aware of efforts to transform them, men of the lower mass were deprived of the dignity that had been theirs when they were accepted as virtuous by society's leading elements. They were now asked to feel ashamed of what they had been and were, and to undergo a

1959 1961

SEX
TO
ANI
VER
SA
RIO

complete change in values and attitudes. Moreover, the new liberal approach contributed ultimately, even if unintentionally, to a hardening of racial prejudices, in so far as vice, joined now with poverty, came to be identified with a dark skin.

As a result of circumstances which lead the dominant culture to intrude in a new way upon the sub-culture or to discard time-honoured obligations towards it, a revolution – or an attempt at one – is unlikely to emerge. However complex and veiled its motivation, the revolution will probably initially assume the outer form – reflected by propaganda and sometimes by the sincere utterances of its leaders – of an endeavour to shape the structure of the dominant culture, allegedly corrupted by its liberal, bourgeois ways, in line with the non-capitalist life styles associated with the sub-culture. Revolutionary leadership will, most likely, be provided by alienated members of the dominant culture.

As the threat of social revolution intensifies, the leaders of the prevailing system can save themselves immediately by violent repression. If they are to survive in the long run, on the other hand, they must devise new methods to re-establish more harmonious relations between the two cultures and to restore unity among the different elements of the dominant culture. What follows in the ensuing chapters is the story of the general success of the ruling classes of twentieth-century Spanish America in discovering the long-term methods necessary to calm revolutionary situations, and thereby to preserve tradition.

2 Ideology: The Challenge to and Defence of the Traditional Society

THREE POSITIVIST PHILOSOPHIES

Spanish America's romantic liberals of the immediate post-independence period, irrepressibly optimistic in their appraisal of human nature, had wished to remove restrictions and restraints in society in order to bring an equalitarian state into being. However, as they fell under the influence of positivism in the second half of the nineteenth century, liberals became increasingly pessimistic in assessing the potential of the vast majority of people inhabiting the new republics. Concerned more and more to encourage a natural élite, the liberals-turned-positivists wished to remove restrictions and restraints in society for the benefit of those allegedly fit to profit from the ensuing freedom. Eschewing the paternalism of Auguste Comte's pristine positivism, one important group of positivists accepted the concept of unrestricted struggle, or social Darwinism, associated with Herbert Spencer. The result was a rather unnatural union between the ideologies of Comte and Spencer.

Pensadores (literally, thinkers) such as Antonio García Cubas and Francisco Bulnes in Mexico, the younger Carlos Octavio Bunge and José Ingenieros in Argentina, and Alcides Argüedas, Oyola Cuellar and Nicomedes Antelo in Bolivia insisted upon the inherent racial inferiority of the vast Indian-mestizo-mulatto masses of the national populaces. In their view, the proper way to deal with the Spanish American masses was to stop pampering them in a spirit of paternalism and leave them to die out in an unrestricted struggle with the fitter elements of society. At the same time most of the leading figures who subscribed to this racialist school of thought saw the need to encourage massive immigration from the countries of western Europe that had presumably achieved a more advanced stage in the evolutionary process. Through the immigration of Caucasians they hoped to achieve their paramount goal of national economic development.

In spite of the prevalence of racialist positivism in Mexico, a formidable outcry of protest greeted a suggestion in the *New York Herald* in 1884 that all Indians, being incorrigible, should be exterminated in the interest of progress. The protest, which T. G. Powell described in *The Hispanic American Historical Review* in February 1968, arose in part because of the influence of Gabino Barreda, who had helped to bring into being a different, reformist school of positivism. Barreda and his followers conceded that the Indians, who constituted by far the largest part of Mexico's masses, were inferior in their present state and an impediment to national development. But through better feeding and education, they believed, the Indians could be converted into agents of progress. Basically, they argued that Indians could be reformed by being made self-reliant; they could be infused with ambitions for material, individual gain and then taught how to satisfy their new ambitions by acquiring productive skills and habits of thrift and foresight. The reformist positivists therefore set out to render the Indians worthy and virtuous by turning them into replicas of the individualistic, self-reliant, materialistic, capitalist-oriented elements within the middle and upper classes. One way to initiate the process of reform lay, they believed, in depriving Indian settlements of communal properties and turning each member into a private landowner.

Other Spanish American countries as well as Mexico produced prominent spokesmen for this type of reformism. In Peru, for example, Javier Prado y Ugarteche came to believe that the lower classes, both Indian and non-Indian, could be uplifted and transformed into instruments of national progress. In his book *Estado social del Perú durante la dominación española* (1894), Prado stressed that education must be used to awaken in the individual the desire for greater well-being; material ambition would in turn implant in individuals a higher degree of civic virtue and personal morality. 'It is necessary', he insisted, 'to educate, and to educate through labour, through industry, which is the greatest medium of moralization. There is nothing which will better elevate a man's character today, nothing which will make him interest himself more effectively in the future of his country, than to educate him to be practical and prudent and to acquire wealth by means of his personal efforts.'

A similar position was taken by the Chilean Francisco Antonio Encina when, in his book *Nuestra inferioridad económica* (1912), he complained that the Latin American republics were becoming economic colonies of the United States. This he attributed to the economic inferiority, the lack of capitalist, productive virtues, that typified all too many Latin Americans. Encina demanded a new approach to education, one aimed at instilling in all members of society, from top to bottom, the productive, individualistic, self-reliant capitalist outlook that certain enlightened middle sectors had already acquired.

Whether the reason was the desire of the upper classes to eliminate them, or alternatively, to change and uplift them, the Spanish American masses began to experience new pressures around the turn of the century. Society no longer afforded them a secure and respectable place; it no longer recognized their dignity and virtue within their traditional world of values. These circumstances inevitably fostered bewilderment and resentment. In Mexico the Indian Emiliano Zapata raised the cry *Tierra y Libertad* ('Land and Liberty'), voicing the desire of the masses to regain security in their traditional patterns of collective landownership, to be left alone once more in their accustomed way of life and to regain freedom from the intrusion of an uncongenial world. Zapata also expressed the resentment of the Indians when, in a conversation with Pancho Villa in 1914, he exclaimed: 'Those son-of-a-bitch politicians. . . . I can't stand them. . . . They're all a bunch of bastards.' Much of Zapata's anger stemmed from the manner in which politicians, especially since the 1880s, had intruded into the world of the Indian sub-culture.

In Mexico many members of the ruling classes had also become alienated. Encouraged by the restlessness of the masses, engendered in part by the attempt to reform them on bourgeois lines, they began to raise the call to revolution. Their idea was to use the masses in order to force the upper classes to reform themselves in accordance with the non-capitalist values, traditions and general patterns of life of society's underlings. Not surprisingly, then, Zapata found in an alienated intellectual, Antonio

5 Emiliano Zapata (fifth from the left) and, next to him (in uniform), Pancho Villa, two of the most famous guerrilla leaders of the Mexican Revolution, head a procession of their followers.

Díaz Soto y Gama, a spokesman for a revolutionary change that would involve little less than imposing certain values of the Indian sub-culture upon the middle and upper classes. And in Chile, where Indians had long since been virtually eliminated, Luis Emilio Recabarren responded in a somewhat similar manner to the perplexity and resentment of the urban lower classes as the dominant groups either intensified their exploitation or insisted that the lower classes begin to emulate their betters. By the early 1920s Recabarren was preaching a revolution that would bring all society into line with the allegedly socialist, collectivist, non-capitalist, non-materialistic values of the masses.

Throughout Spanish America the old live-and-let-live relationship between the dominant and the sub-cultures was beginning to break down. The ruling classes had initiated the process by intruding more forcefully into the lives of the masses. The resulting tensions produced a favourable climate for numerous revolutionaries, among them radical socialists and anarchists, whose aim was to impose the values of the sub-culture upon the world of the dominant culture, and so, in fact, to destroy it.

Except in Mexico – and later in Bolivia and Cuba – the pressures generated by the ruling classes were decreased in the course of time and the potential for revolution was reduced. As a result the traditional society survived essentially intact. Just as some ideological factors had contributed to the creation of a revolutionary situation, so others helped to contain it by providing an intellectual climate conducive to preserving the established order.

A third group of intellectuals – the paternalistic positivists – always stressed social harmony and order above progress. They realized instinctively that national development based upon awakening the competitive instincts and materialistic aspirations of the masses portended the collapse of the traditional society. Their aim was to prevent such a collapse by inducing the masses to accept their place in a pattern of existence characterized by dependence, and in this way to defuse the revolutionary situation. Hence they called upon the privileged classes to assume new paternalistic obligations that would ensure social solidarity by guaranteeing economic security to the lower orders. At the same time the paternalistic positivists sought to provide the masses with non-material rewards that would afford them spiritual contentment within their lowly economic status. In spiritual gratification combined with paternalistic protection, they saw the means of restoring a harmonious relationship among the various components of society.

This type of self-interested paternalism was proclaimed in Argentina by J. Alfredo Ferreira in an article published in the periodical *La Escuela Positiva* in 1899. Communism, Ferreira wrote, had played an understandable role in helping to awaken the labouring classes and to expand their horizons, but it was not acceptable as an ultimate solution to the social problem. Rather, the solution lay in a form of positivism that stressed the social duties of property. A similar approach was developed in Chile by Valentín Letelier, who defeated Enrique Mac-Iver, an advocate of Spencerian positivism, in the councils of the Chilean Radical Party in 1907; and from that time onwards the country's Radicals paid lip service to a form of government intervention in social questions which they described as socialism.

In Bolivia certain *pensadores*, among them Ignacio Prudencio Bustillo, began to urge that the state respect the distinctive features of Indian culture, including collective landownership, even though these features might not be conducive to material development in line with scientific laws of progress. And in Venezuela intellectuals such as Gil Fortoul and, later and far more directly, Laureano Vallenilla Lanz argued the case for paternalistic dictatorship, expressing doubt whether much could be accomplished in the way of reforming the masses.

The paternalistic positivists were not particularly concerned if the social costs of their programmes slowed the rate of economic development. They accepted this overhead as necessary to preserve social solidarity and order, without which there could be no long-term, sustained material development. What attracted them was the vision of an ideal society that had many points of similarity to that of the colonial period. Within this society – new, yet rooted in the past – the possibilities for overall economic development would be limited by the inability of the masses to acquire extensive purchasing power. The advantage of this society was that within it the directing classes would remain unchallenged because the masses were shielded against ambitions for economic, material self-reliance – ambitions that if fulfilled would give rise to demands for social and political independence.

In seeking to give the masses non-material rewards and incentives so as to preserve social harmony, Spanish American paternalistic philosophers borrowed heavily from the teachings of a writer who, through his disciples, had an enormous posthumous influence on Spanish liberalism and positivism in the second half of the nineteenth century: Karl Christian Friedrich Krause.

The best-known Spanish translation of a work by Krause, *Ideal de la humanidad para la vida* (1860), reveals most of the essential features of his social philosophy. In it Krause lays down that every individual is placed on earth to pursue his end through his particular vocation. Moreover, however lowly his estate, each man should participate to some degree in 'the higher callings of human nature'. Thus, members of all social classes should be taught to appreciate the beauty of their physical surroundings and given a liberal education, including instruction in art, literature and music, intended to awaken in them a regard for the aesthetic world. By learning to perceive, however dimly, and to appreciate, however imperfectly, the higher truths and beauties of life, men would be liberated from obsession with material desires, from base passions and appetites, from selfish inclinations and resentment and rancour against others. Thus liberated, they would achieve a harmonious and fully developed character, while at the same time finding the solace and joys necessary to make them content and resigned in the stations in life to which they were called.

As they began in their limited way to interest themselves in the higher things of life the humble classes, according to Krause and his Spanish as well as his Spanish American disciples, would come to revere the hierarchy of values in which the artistic and spiritual and aesthetic took precedence over material considerations. They would come to revere this hierarchy because in their leisure time, when they enjoyed respite from the physical labour that gave 'no nourishment to the spirit and that chilled the heart', they would find an exhilarating and rewarding world in the higher pleasures to which they had been introduced by their liberal education. Coming to appreciate a hierarchy of values, the labouring classes would tolerate and even welcome the existing social hierarchy, understanding that only better men were capable of fruitfully pursuing the better things in life and achieving new works of artistic creativity that would eventually add to the pleasure of the humble, non-creative classes.

The Argentinian positivist Manuel A. Bermudes clearly identified himself with the Krausist approach when he argued in 1897 in his article 'Educación y socialismo' that through education the poor and humble could be made to understand that their situation was natural and that they could thereby be liberated from resentment against the rich and the mighty. In order to achieve this purpose, Bermudes affirmed, education had not merely to be vocational; it had also to be liberal, so as to acquaint the student with the wonders of the realms of the mind and soul.

ARIELISM

The champions of paternalistic, harmonious positivism hoped to spiritualize both the masses and, at the same time, a bourgeoisie which was growing all too assertive within the dominant culture; they were also interested in the long-range economic development of their countries and inclined to believe that the laws of progress could be discovered through science. On the other hand they feared the social upheavals that might result from an exclusive obsession with development in the immediate future. In contrast, a new group of intellectuals, the Arielists, who appeared at the turn of the century, were vitally concerned with preserving the traditional social order and entertained considerable doubts about the value of national material development, questioning scientific methodology in general.

Arielism took its name from the book *Ariel*, written by the Uruguayan intellectual José Enrique Rodó and published in 1900. In this work, which became vastly influential throughout the Spanish-speaking world, Rodó depicted Ariel as the creature of intellectual and spiritual pursuits, concerned with art, beauty and moral development as ends in themselves, rather than with material progress. Ariel was used to symbolize what, for Rodó, was most authentic in Hispanic culture. Through the words he gave to Ariel, the author chided Spanish Americans, sometimes directly, sometimes by implication, for having abandoned the culture and values natural to them and having embraced the materialistic, utilitarian, mechanistic life styles associated with alien cultures, most specifically with Anglo-Saxon civilization.

Arielism coincided with and contributed to the growing hostility to the United States at the turn of the century, provoked by a fear of Yankee imperialism. To fear of political and economic imperialism, Arielism added a cultural dimension. Basic to the Arielist position was the conviction that the type of culture developed by Yankees would, if allowed to penetrate Spanish America, contribute to levelling social revolutions. Out of this

6 *No Other Arm Around This Waist!* A *Harper's Weekly* cartoon of 1900 expresses the Yankee cultural dominance feared by many Spanish Americans.

NO OTHER ARM AROUND THIS WAIST!

conviction came the resolute determination of many Spanish Americans to return to and strengthen their own unique cultural traditions, to reassert their own specific national identities and immunize themselves against United States influence.

The basic flaw in United States culture, according to most Arielists and to the proponents of paternalistic, spiritual positivism as well, lay in its exclusive concern with the material development and progress of the individual and the nation. Only a materialistic society, they contended, could accept the madness of political democracy based upon the concept of one man, one vote. A materialistic society was characterized by an obsessive interest in things; because all men were capable of producing and consuming things – though not ideas – such a society granted them an equal political voice. Within a materialistic society whose hallmark was indifference to the provinces of mind and soul, it seemed suitable enough to permit, through the operation of egalitarian democracy, the destruction of the social hierarchies essential to preserving the hierarchy of values.

Within the United States proper, in the view of many Arielists and their ideological associates, some element of social solidarity and political stability could be maintained. A people by nature materialistic, as Yankees were assumed to be, could achieve institutional stability within a democratic order permeated throughout by individualistic, capitalist values. Such a people, of course, could never amount to much in the overall scale of human values. They could contribute little to art, to the spiritual development of men, to the nobler creations of which the human spirit was capable. They could, however, achieve remarkable results on the lower levels of human existence and in general satisfy the wants of a materialistic citizenry sufficiently to prevent anarchy and chronic disorder.

The real importance of the Arielists, however, lies in their analysis of Spanish America. They insisted that the transfer of the materialistic approach to life to a people and a cultural milieu marked by an overriding concern with the higher, more spiritual values of human existence, and accordingly organized in hierarchical fashion, must inevitably undermine the established order and pose the threat of social revolution. In their view the materialistic concept of life was fundamentally incompatible with one that was spiritual and humanistic; it could establish itself only by destroying the institutions and social order that had naturally developed in response to the needs and aspirations of a society that put intangible benefits first. Thus, when Spanish Americans denied their own nature and cultural identity, when they introduced democratic experiments and sought to disseminate throughout society the alien values of acquisitive, competitive, individualistic capitalism, they were, however unwittingly, serving the cause of social revolution.

As a result of the Plenary Council of Latin American prelates, convoked in Rome by Pope Leo XIII in 1899, came an effort to reinvigorate the Church in Latin America and to improve its channels of communication with the Vatican. The Plenary Council also gave rise to a series of provincial councils within the various Latin American republics, one of the first of which was held in Caracas in 1904. The resurgence of the Catholic Church in Venezuela, dating from this provincial council, continued during the long dictatorship of Juan Vicente Gómez (1908–35).

The Plenary Council was also followed by a number of provincial councils in Colombia. The third of these, held in Bogotá in 1916, produced a joint pastoral in which the prelates instructed the faithful to vote only for political leaders who would protect the interests of the Church and allow the clergy a role of 'moderate intervention' in the public life of the country. At the conclusion of the council a Spanish journalist writing in the Jesuit organ *Razón y Fe* in January 1917 complimented the bishops for their efforts which had, he said, increased the already appreciable strength of the Church in Colombia and established it as the most formidable 'bulwark of the existing social order'.

7 A Roman Catholic missionary from Spain preaching to a group of Perahija Indians in Venezuela.

The Church's gradual acquisition of prestige and influence in Venezuela, following a period of rampant anti-clericalism in the late nineteenth century, and the strengthening of its already considerable power in Colombia were signs of a general revival of Catholic influence in most parts of Spanish America. In an indirect way the resurgence of Catholicism can be traced back to the reaction of Arielism at the turn of the century against materialism and mechanistic utilitarianism. It is true that Arielism, initiated by men like Rodó who were indifferent to religion, shared with positivism a hearty, sometimes even a virulent, anti-clericalism. Both Arielists and paternalistic, spiritual positivists believed that humanism afforded an adequate foundation upon which to base the higher values they extolled. But roughly between 1910 and 1930 – though the situation differed considerably from country to country – a new pattern became discernible. Increasingly the leaders of the spiritual reaction against utilitarian and materialistic criteria began to return to the Catholic Church, persuaded that the higher human values, if they were to prevail against democratic, levelling, revolutionary impulses, required a basis in theology and revelation. The famous Peruvian intellectual José de la Riva Agüero stands as a symbol of this development. In his youth a leader of the Peruvian version of the Arielist movement and strongly influenced by liberal anti-clericalism, Riva Agüero made a conspicuous return to the Catholic Church in 1932.

Not all countries, of course, shared to an equal degree in this type of cultural change. In Mexico, where after the Revolution of 1910 intellectuals preferred to flirt with radical anti-clerical and sometimes atheistic doctrines, and in Uruguay, where the Church had never enjoyed more than a tenuous existence and where agnosticism was a significant intellectual force, the reaction against materialism failed to evolve into a major resurgence of Catholic influence. Even in Mexico, however, by the late 1920s José Vasconcelos and, more clearly still, Alfonso Junco typified a growing number of *pensadores* who emerged as apologists for Hispanic traditions, including Catholicism; and in the 1930s the ultra-Catholic *sinarquista* movement gained a large mass following among rural Mexicans as well as the backing of some intellectuals. Meanwhile, moreover, the Uruguayan Luis Alberto de Herrera was developing into perhaps the most eloquent lay spokesman of traditional Catholic values that his country has produced.

Early in the twentieth century, the Spanish American episcopacy launched an effort to organize the laity into Catholic Action, hoping thereby to capitalize on the increasingly favourable circumstances in which they found themselves and at the same time to ease social tensions. The primary purposes of Catholic Action were to win back the masses to the faith and to quicken the social conscience of the upper classes so as to induce them, under the hierarchy's supervision, to take paternalistic measures to mitigate the suffering and isolation of the masses. This little-studied development in Spanish American Catholicism undoubtedly helped to dissipate the pressures for revolutionary change.

Catholic spokesmen attributed the mounting social tensions in Spanish America to the secularization of society that had been under way since the eighteenth century. Unlike those positivists influenced by Krause, they denied that the masses could be persuaded through education and an appeal to reason alone to accept their inequality on this earth. Only when convinced of their equality in a life to come would they resign themselves to a temporal status of inequality. It followed, then, that all those who advocated secularism, among them liberals, positivists and the early Arielists, were, however contrary to their intentions, preparing the way for social revolution.

The spectre of social revolution contributed to a *rapprochement* between anti-clericals and proponents of Catholic social doctrines. Faced with what appeared to be an immediate threat to the established order, anti-clericals began to curb their demands for the total secularization of society and to present a common front with religious leaders against the forces of change. Even during the late nineteenth century Bolivia's traditionally anti-clerical Liberals had managed to arrive at a mutually advantageous *modus vivendi* with the Church-affiliated Conservatives. By the late 1920s this pattern had established itself in Colombia, where the Liberals, out of office at the time, discovered a basis of co-operation with the incumbent Conservatives. By the early 1930s Chilean Liberals and Conservatives, discounting the issues that had divided them for decades, had joined together to form an alliance that would remain one of the country's most powerful political forces for the next thirty years.

CORPORATIVE DECENTRALIZATION

Most Catholic observers of Spanish America at the turn of the century, and a good number of ardent secularists as well, expressed alarm at the degree to which the masses were becoming alienated from a social and political system that did not even permit them a minimal degree of participation. They also pointed with apprehension to a situation in which individual members of the labouring classes no longer enjoyed a secure sanctuary in society but were constrained to compete for their livelihood under conditions that rendered their chances of success minimal. To remedy this situation, which if ignored might result in revolution, they urged the decentralized and corporative organization of society. Their programme called for breaking down the monolithic, centralized social-political structure into its natural subdivisions (organisms or corporations) and granting to the masses some voice in governing the subdivisions appropriate to them.

Spanish American Catholics recognized at an early date what Erich Fromm later called the inherent contradiction between competition and 'belongingness'. In restoring to the masses of society a sense of belongingness, Catholic *pensadores* hoped to avoid social revolution. In their analysis they even found common ground with Karl Marx, although their prescriptions for the future differed in all respects from his. Marx saw corporative institutions as one of the means whereby social harmony had been maintained in medieval Europe; and he contended that the separation, specification and division of labour basic to industrial capitalism produced an estrangement in human relations that led to the fragmentation of society at all levels. It was precisely this fragmentation that alarmed Catholic thinkers and led them to advocate a return to the corporative structure.

According to its Catholic critics, the liberal, secular state – excessively individualistic and at the same time excessively centralized – had eliminated the possibility of hierarchical organization. Within such a state each individual operated as a free atom, participated by his vote in decisions at all levels, and was allowed and even encouraged to raise his voice on issues he was incapable of understanding. The democratic goals of this unnatural organization were seen as self-defeating. Eventually, most individuals, because of their inherent inability to understand the complex issues of national policy on which their votes were solicited, would retreat into their own narrow world of self-interest and abandon all concern with the republic. The Catholic advocates of decentralization argued that by replacing an atomistic with an organic or corporative structure it would be possible for each individual to find his way into a local political group, and in addition into a professional or functional organization, in the management of which he could safely and knowledgeably participate. Content within their own sphere of activity and active politically to the fullest extent their faculties permitted, the masses would happily leave decision-making on the higher, national level to an élite that would emerge through careful screening procedures.

By means of corporative decentralization Catholics hoped not only to preserve the hierarchical social order but also gradually to desecularize society. They envisaged the organization of labour and professional groups under strict Church dominance, relatively free from the control of a centralized state bureaucracy, which in their view was often tainted by liberal, secular, anti-clerical, materialistic, Masonic errors, by Jewish and Marxist aberrations and even by Protestant heresies. In the final analysis,

Spanish American Catholics tended to see excessive centralism arising from the same heretical assumptions that allegedly underlay democracy. They contended that from the heretical premise of the equality of all men – said to be an outgrowth, even if unforeseen, of the individualistic Protestant approach to religion – there had followed the conclusion that all citizens should be ruled by the same laws and institutions. As a result all local and regional 'particularisms' had been repressed by a despotic central government that absorbed or eliminated all intermediary associations between itself and its citizens.

Many positivists and Arielists, and also members of other anti-clerical and secularist groups, concurred with Catholic spokesmen on the desirability of a decentralized state that would alleviate revolutionary pressures by providing for popular political participation at the level of professional or local corporations. Still, however much inclined they may have been as the twentieth century advanced to co-operate with Catholics in waging a common struggle against basic social change, secularists were not prepared to accept any form of decentralization that increased the Catholic Church's temporal influence unnecessarily. This situation led to a split within the ranks of the secularist defenders of the *status quo*. Some continued to urge decentralization, but a large number decided to work through the existing centralized state structure over which anti-clerical forces had gained control in most republics – a control which by and large they continued to maintain despite the twentieth-century resurgence of Catholic influence.

To a considerable extent, therefore, partisans of secularism abandoned the corporative cause to Catholics, opting instead for a centralized, nation-wide, state controlled system of paternalistic government administered by a secular bureaucracy. Such a system had the disadvantage of denying to the masses such satisfaction as comes from participating in the decisions of subsidiary corporations within the body politic. On the other hand, it was believed that a centralized, paternalistic government would stifle revolutionary impulses by guaranteeing economic security to the masses, thereby increasing their attachment to the established political and social system. Furthermore, they might be given a sense of dignity and participation if effectively persuaded that they were playing an essential role in advancing national progress. In this way a new secular religion of nationalism might take the place of traditional Catholicism and provide the spiritual, non-material gratifications required to make the masses content to remain within their customary place in society.

In all these ways – by means of a secular, liberal education or a religious revival, by private or state controlled paternalism, by decentralization or through a highly centralized structure whose existence was justified by an appeal to nationalism – the dominant classes of Spanish America hoped to keep the masses dependent and isolate them from the values of *laissez-faire* capitalism and individualistic materialism. If assured of economic security, if given non-material rewards in the form of art or religion, or participation in subsidiary groups natural and appropriate to them, or if they could be persuaded that they were playing a role in realizing their nation's destiny, the dependent classes would presumably not demand a revolutionary departure from the uses of the past. Instead, they would remain content within a system that took from them according to their abilities and gave to them according to their needs. They would remain, in short, basically non-capitalist. And they would tolerate the continued existence above them of a culture which was capitalist, at least in so far as its members expected from the system a great deal more than the satisfaction of their basic needs. In such circumstances, tradition would be secure.

3 Social and Economic Factors in Preserving the Traditional Society

The old system of paternalism in Spanish America, established in colonial times and reflecting in many ways the institutions of central and southern Spain, began to collapse in the nineteenth century. One reason for this can be traced to the declining power of the Church at that time. Buffeted in most republics by an onslaught of hard-hitting anti-clerical legislation, the Church lost the lands on which it had provided security for large numbers of peasant labourers. It lost also the capital resources and income that had enabled it in colonial times and at the outset of the independence period to be the main supporter of charitable programmes.

More significant in causing the disruption of the old paternalism was a population shift away from the countryside into the cities, a shift that got under way in most Spanish American republics in the late nineteenth century. Some of the migrating rural masses were Indians whose communal properties had been seized in the name of liberal reform. The majority were peasants – both Indian and non-Indian, depending on the country – who had laboured on large, privately owned rural estates. By migrating these rural masses passed directly from a manorial setting – in which they had been cared for paternalistically, had never learned to protect themselves in a competitive society and had almost never acquired an education – into new conditions of incipient industrial urban life. Moreover, the recent arrivals in the cities knew nothing of how to organize to protect their interests. Emerging urban capitalists would have been more than human had they initially exhibited a spirit of *noblesse oblige* similar to that which had prevailed in employer-employee relationships in a rural setting. Inevitably these circumstances produced a reaction as the burgeoning urban proletariat, responding with mounting enthusiasm to revolutionary rhetoric, began to show signs of striking back at an exploitative system.

From the early twentieth century governments took action to calm the discontent of urban masses – their numbers dramatically swelled in such countries as Argentina and Uruguay by foreign immigrants – by extending to them vast new concessions, including employer liability protection, accident and unemployment insurance, and virtual guarantees against dismissal, almost regardless of inefficiency and provocation to management. Workers were also provided with medical clinics, somewhat better working conditions, sports fields, parks, subsidized housing, concerts, cheap holidays and excursions, as well as lavish spectacles and parades on literally dozens of holidays; and the prices for the more popular, mass-consumed alcoholic drinks were maintained at an incredibly low level. By and large, however, workers did not receive substantial increases in real wages. An increase in real wages would have brought genuine power to the masses, whereas generous grants of fringe benefits left them dependent upon, and hopefully grateful to, the system that furnished the benefits. The masses remained, therefore, essentially a sub-culture, free from the spirit of self-reliance assured by individual control over capital surpluses.

The inflationary process in most Spanish American republics, reaching back in many instances as far as the late nineteenth century, also had the effect of maintaining the masses in a condition of dependence – by chance, probably, rather than design. Conditions of spiralling inflation discouraged the lower classes from acquiring the habits of thrift and saving through which, in a stable economy, they could have gained economic independence. They remained instead dependent upon the government to provide

8 Holiday parade in the Great Square, Montevideo, in the early years of the twentieth century.

them at periodic intervals with cost-of-living adjustments which, while possibly compensating for losses in purchasing power caused by inflation, did not constitute an increment in real wages.

Many critics of the Spanish American ruling classes have suggested that the masses have been betrayed by the system on which they depend; it is arguable, however, that given the economic resources available to them, Spanish American governments have been proportionately more generous in dealing with the lower classes than the governments of many advanced economic powers. Through a new paternalism devised early in the century, Spanish America's urban proletariat has been spared at least some aspects of the brutal exploitation that characterized the industrial revolution in England, the United States and, for that matter, in Communist Russia. The degree of protection in Spanish America has conceivably impeded industrialization. But it has served the cause that is dearer to most Spanish American leadership groups: the preservation of the traditional, two-culture society. In this process, Spanish America discarded liberal political theory and moved back towards the political traditions of the past; a paternalistic, all-embracing central government re-emerged as the dominant factor in national politics.

In implementing vast and complex new programmes of paternalism, Spanish American states relied extensively upon government controlled labour unions. Labour leaders were absorbed into the established system and assigned the role of intermediaries between the rank and file union membership and the government. Their success in serving their constituencies depended upon their ability to wrest favours from the government for which they acted virtually as bureaucrats. Finding it expedient to abandon policies of militant confrontation with capital, a great number of union leaders happily settled for the benefits they could gain by maintaining a friendly working relationship with the political masters of their countries. Labour leaders thus co-opted were no more inclined to rise against governments in which they had a vital stake than were the major-domos on the large *haciendas* of colonial times to strike out against the estate owners whom, with advantage, they served. Some labour leaders, of course, resolutely refused to work within the established system. Espousing revolutionary ideals, especially those of socialism and anarchism, they sought to dismantle the traditional order. In most countries, however, their influence remained relatively slight and they were eclipsed by those leaders who had been co-opted.

MIDDLE SECTORS IN A TWO-CULTURE SOCIETY
Judged by purely economic criteria, a substantial middle class came into existence in Spanish America during the first half of the twentieth century.

31

But, notwithstanding important divisions and cleavages, the various sectors of the middle class identified by and large with the upper classes (widely referred to, especially by critics, as the *oligarquía*), reflected their values, imitated their customs and patterns of behaviour and looked forward some day to entering their ranks. While they were waiting to enjoy a higher status, they did all in their power to safeguard the perquisites, privileges and immunities of the upper-class world so that its splendours would be undiminished when they finally rose into it. As a result, in spite of the emergence of sectors that on economic grounds have to be denominated middle class, Spanish America remained psychologically and in values and attitudes a two-culture society. For a time, it is true, at a point early in the twentieth century, an assertive bourgeoisie seemed as though it might impose its values throughout society. But when it became apparent that this could lead to a revolutionary situation, the bourgeois elements curbed their efforts to reform the sub-culture and at the same time reverted to their position as defenders, rather than modifiers, of upper-class life styles and values. Because of the general reluctance of Spanish America's bourgeoisie – at least until some time in the second half of the twentieth century – to regard themselves as members of a permanently distinct class, they are referred to most often in this book as middle sectors rather than as a middle class.

One factor explaining the attitudes of the middle sectors is that historically Spanish America's aristocracy (for the sake of simplicity, albeit at the sacrifice of total accuracy, the term is used synonymously with upper classes) has remained relatively open to new members. Thus it was by no means unrealistic for members of the middle sectors to look forward to climbing into the aristocracy. Throughout the nineteenth and early twentieth centuries many old and established aristocratic landowning families, heavily in debt because of the uneconomic management of their estates, welcomed alliances, often cemented through marriage, with affluent men of urban, industrial and commercial backgrounds. Once they had acquired the social status reserved in the Hispanic world to landownership, the fresh arrivals in upper-class families frequently abandoned their old business pursuits, now considered beneath their dignity, and took to the established aristocracy's uneconomic way of life. As a result within a generation or two the new aristocrats found themselves in their turn in financial distress that could best be relieved by opening their ranks, again often through marriage, to a new generation of successful bourgeois capitalists.

This ever-recurring process, which had already become firmly established in the seventeenth-century colonial period, contributed significantly to social stability and to the preservation of the two-culture society. At the same time, it drained money from capital-generating urban enterprise and

9 The aristocratic lady of the manor: portrait of the Argentinian Señora Elvira Lavalleja de Calzadilla by Prilidiano Pueyrredón.

channelled it into largely non-productive investments. The typical land-owner in the Hispanic world regarded his real estate as a badge of social prestige and as a source of money for conspicuous consumption rather than as a means to bring about the growth of capital.

In order that the traditional society should remain secure, it was not enough for men of the middle sectors to cling to the dream of ascent to aristocratic status. They had, in addition, to be given sufficient means to allow them to wait in dignity and also to act, in many respects, as if they had already joined the upper-class world. A dramatic proliferation of the bureaucracy helped to create these conditions. Government salaries, as well as the many opportunities for graft that offered themselves to state functionaries, presented bureaucrats with the financial means to emulate the aristocracy's conspicuous consumption without having to lower themselves to money-grubbing, economically productive occupations.

The effects of an unnecessarily large bureaucracy whose corruption was almost institutionalized militated against economic development, while contributing to social stability. In all of this there was little that was fundamentally new. In the Hispanic world of the sixteenth and seventeenth centuries, in much of the peninsula and in the American colonies, a mushrooming bureaucracy, combined with opportunities for frequent new admissions into the titled and lesser nobility, had served to maintain the established social order. At the same time these circumstances had helped to produce economic stagnation.

Expansion of education further served to buttress the *status quo*. One of the most enduring and consequential effects of the University Reform movement that exploded in 1918 in Córdoba (Argentina), and simultaneously in other parts of Spanish America, was the opening of institutions

10 Indian children learning arithmetic from an abacus in a school in Andean Bolivia.

of higher education to many middle-sector youths who had previously been excluded. Hereafter, more and more men of middle economic status had the chance to attend a university and acquire the law degree that was all important for gaining a post in the government bureaucracy or in other occupations that did not carry the social stigma attached to direct involvement in the primary, productive sector of the economy. Moreover, expansion of educational facilities below the university level, to which many republics devoted considerable expenditure from the beginning of the century onwards, helped to cement the loyalty of the lower classes.

The schools provided in increasing numbers for lower-class children were, of course, staffed by men and women who were products of the dominant culture – largely middle-sector individuals who identified with upper-class values. They knew little if anything of the life and style of the sub-culture from which the bulk of their students came. Speaking in terms that did not bridge the gulf separating the two cultures, the teachers failed to educate. Consequently a high percentage of children in the elementary public schools failed their courses. If they persevered in the school system, they were likely to repeat the lower two or three grades year after year. Their parents, grateful to the government for having presented them with the novel experience of sending their children to school, attributed the failure of their offspring to natural stupidity – many of the children actually were mentally retarded, not necessarily as a result of genetic factors but because of the high incidence of injuries at birth among the poor, malnutrition, sickness and accidents during the earliest years of life. In this process lower-class parents became all the more resigned to allowing men of presumed intelligence to direct affairs of state.

Richard M. Morse has provided a profound insight into the effects of the middle-sector orientation of the public school curricula in the rural zone of Córdoba, and his analysis may legitimately be extended to cover much of pre-university public education throughout the rest of Spanish America. As Morse puts it, 'The failure of children in school, a most frequent occurrence, [signified] the victory of community integration.' In other words, the failed child was drawn back into his own cultural community, becoming thereby more fully than ever integrated into what the present study describes as a sub-culture.

THE DOMINANT CULTURE, INDUSTRIALIZATION AND THE MONEY OF POWER

The process of upward social mobility which siphoned men out of commerce and industry and projected them into an economically non-productive realm interfered with the continuity of economic development in

35

Spanish America. Certainly it slowed the rate of industrialization in most of the republics during the period from 1900 to the 1950s. At certain points in the twentieth century, however, when the flow of manufactured goods from the world's economically developed countries was interrupted, Spanish American republics were forced to introduce massive import substitution programmes. This was particularly so at the time of the First World War, when because of military involvement the leading world powers could no longer supply Spanish America with finished products, and again during the years of the great depression, when the area was unable to finance the importation of manufactured goods owing to low world prices for its raw products.

During these times of crisis Spanish American governments had to counteract ingrained social prejudices against industrial entrepreneurship and to cajole men with surplus capital into becoming industrialists. In the process, governments resorted to monopolistic concessions, tax exemptions, tariff protection and other privileges and incentives. The resulting industrial élite owed its existence and opportunities for future aggrandizement to government. In a way, the new industrialists were as dependent upon government as the leaders of organized labour. Furthermore, their emergence, like that of labour leaders, did not pose a challenge to the established system of which government was a servant, but instead strengthened that system.

Claudio Véliz, the Chilean historian, has pointed out that in England and much of western Europe industrialization was the marginal result of a new way of life, a part of a complex cultural whole which included attitudes towards art and literature, education, and also public and private morality. An industrial bourgeoisie identifying with the new cultural values challenged tradition and triumphed. In contrast to the spontaneous, natural process of industrialization in much of the western world, the unnatural, forced industrialization of Spanish America perpetuated the existing social structure.

Véliz's analysis may be supplemented by that which the Spanish intellectual and statesman Ramiro de Maeztu developed in the *Revista de las Españas* in 1927. Fascinated throughout his life by the differences between Spanish and Anglo-Saxon culture (both his mother and wife were English and he lived for many years in England), Maeztu argued that English-speaking men generally sought the power of money, while, by contrast, in the Hispanic world both Spaniards and Spanish Americans pursued the money of power. By this Maeztu meant that Anglo Saxons were inclined unabashedly to throw themselves into economic enterprise and, having thereby acquired money, to exult in the individual power that it gave them. On the other hand, in the Hispanic world there was a tendency to avoid involvement in direct economic enterprise which, it was believed, dehumanized people and stifled appreciation of higher aesthetic and cultural values. When in quest of money the typical product of Hispanic culture turned to those in power in government and garnered concessions from them that assured economic success without really having to work for it. Such a person was concerned with the money of power.

This approach seems to have been deeply ingrained in Hispanic, especially Castilian, culture. Ideally, according to its standards, money, like happiness, is not to be won in direct pursuit. When it comes, well and good: it is the result of benign providence or of *buena suerte* (good luck). Acquired in this way, money can confer honour and distinction, whereas if it is accumulated through direct pursuit it attests to a person's greed.

In the realm of traditional Castilian values, within which, in spite of frequent protestations to the contrary, the New World's Spanish-speaking republics largely continue to function, the prosperous capitalist feels constrained to apologize for his success. He can do so by attempting to demonstrate that his wealth came not from seeking it directly in demeaning economic enterprise but instead was the product of good fortune. The corrupt bureaucrat can acquire a fortune in dignity by using the power of his office, asking all to believe that his financial success is the result of fortuitous circumstances, not of personal acquisitiveness. The prosperous industrialist whose wealth depends on favours from those in power rather than on direct and avaricious pursuit of money can also justify his affluence on the grounds that it is all simply a matter of luck that is very surprising to him. In the Anglo-Saxon world, on the other hand, the capitalist who amasses a fortune through his connections with the wielders of political power tries to mask the fact and to pretend that his success resulted from indefatigable enterprise in the conscious quest of money.

Possession of capital is of course vitally important to members of the dominant culture in Spanish America. Capital provides them with the economic basis for independence, for the individualism and self-reliance that are badges of gentlemanly status. Beyond this, capital is essential if one is to seek fulfilment in the world of aesthetic pleasure and artistic creativity. It is indispensable, moreover, if a man is to prove he is not covetous by indulging in conspicuous consumption, lavish display and all the various acts of prodigality which within the Hispanic culture have traditionally been taken as signs of virtue.

Once the bourgeois assertiveness of the turn of the century had been bridled, Spanish American governments succeeded remarkably in providing men of the dominant culture, whether they were of true upper-class status or only psychologically members of the upper class while economically of the middle level, with the sort of world they desired. The rewards of successful capitalists were made available to them without their having to acquire the skills and attitudes commonly considered pre-requisite for the creation and accumulation of wealth.

Meanwhile, the masses were pacified by a system of fringe benefits that left them thoroughly dependent upon a *patrón* sector and at the same time economically inefficient and non-productive. Because the new pater-nalism saddled government with huge burdens of social expenditure, a considerable price naturally had to be paid for the pacification of the masses.

How could a two-culture society endure economically when its survival seemed to depend upon pampering the semi-capitalists of the dominant culture with all the fruits generally reserved for fully fledged capitalists? How could it endure economically when concomitantly its survival seemed to depend upon preventing the masses from acquiring the capitalist mentality and aspiring to become independent by husbanding capital surpluses? For many years foreign capital in Spanish America played an important role, often totally unperceived by foreign capitalists, in preserv-ing a social structure that economically was not viable.

FOREIGN CAPITAL AND THE PRESERVATION OF THE TRADITIONAL SOCIETY

In their endeavour to conserve the sort of social structure inherited from the colonial past, the privileged classes in Spanish America sensed that they could combine their traditional ideals and values with the advantages of foreign capital. Instinctively, they rejected the validity of the dichotomy presented by Ramón Valle-Inclán in his novel *Tirano Banderas*, published in 1922. In this work the distinguished Spanish writer sketched a scene in which a member of the Spanish colony in a mythical Spanish American country conversed with a United States businessman. The Spaniard insisted that the ruling classes realized that in order to avoid social upheaval they had 'to turn their eyes once more towards the *madre patria*' and steep themselves in its social, economic and ethical values and traditions. With considerable scorn the Yankee businessman replied: 'If the *criollo* [white, Spanish-origin] elements survive as the directing classes it will be owing to the ships and cannons of North America.'

Whether by intuition or conscious rational analysis, Spanish Americans understood that preservation of their social system required both of the elements alluded to by Valle-Inclán. It depended not only upon bolstering the ideals and values of the *madre patria* but also upon the capital and tech-nology of the United States.

To begin with, the social services – by means of which Spanish American governments won the allegiance of the labouring classes, or at least bought their quiescence – had to be financed. As the new paternalism developed and ramified, soaring social overheads seriously reduced the capital that might otherwise have been available for economic development. Had the pressures for investment in economic development not been relieved by foreign capital, Spanish American governments would probably not have been able to fund their social programmes.

For many years, moreover, taxes collected on foreign business allowed the Spanish American élite to remain virtually free from direct taxation; thus the traditions of the colonial period and of pre-conquest Spain were maintained, according to which freedom from many forms of direct taxation was a perquisite of aristocratic status. The propensity of Latin American governments to compel foreign, especially North American, subsidiaries to pay a disproportionately large share of the area's public revenue – even though the sums initially exacted were relatively modest – is indicated in a study entitled *United States Business Investments in Foreign Countries*, published in 1960 by the United States Department of Commerce. According to this, United States companies, while employing a little over 1 per cent of the labour force in Latin America (Brazil included), account for roughly 10 per cent of the area's gross national product and pay one-fifth of all taxes and one-third of all direct assessments on income.

The period immediately following the First World War witnessed an enormous increase in the importance of United States capital within the Spanish American economies. It was then that North Americans achieved the long cherished goal of taking over the role originally played by British, and to a lesser extent by German, Italian and French investors and lenders. The extent of United States economic penetration is revealed by statistics.

11 Uruguayan branch of General Motors, the United States automobile manufacturers, in the 1920s.

Between 1919 and 1929, United States investment, direct and indirect, in the five Bolivarian republics (Venezuela, Colombia, Ecuador, Peru and Bolivia) increased from $10 million to $316 million. Between 1920 and 1929, United States direct investment in Chile rose from roughly $200 million to $592 million. Furthermore, in the 1920s, when many Spanish American republics were setting up the machinery of the new paternalism, foreign loans were in abundant supply. In Peru, for example, foreign indebtedness soared from approximately $10 million to $100 million between 1918 and 1929, and most of the foreign loans were obtained from international banking firms incorporated in the United States.

Foreign loans, foreign investment and taxation of foreign business, as well as deficit financing, enabled the Spanish American governing classes to avoid social upheaval while maintaining the traditional ideals bequeathed by the *madre patria*. In order to remain loyal to these ideals, however, the élite had to accept dependence on the capital and technological expertise of the United States.

The result was that Spanish America's dominant culture, while continuing to be dominant *vis-à-vis* the sub-culture, became in turn a sub-culture in relation to United States and other foreign capitalists. Within the Spanish American republics the sub-culture is characterized by a mentality of dependence, by a tendency to live in the present and to avoid preoccupation with accumulating capital to provide for the future; its members are confident that the *patrón*, private or public, will always supply what is required to maintain security in the customary way of life. In its relations to the world of foreign capital, the internally dominant culture of Spanish America showed the same traits. Its members accepted a role of dependence, and in so doing took on the psychological traits that characterize that role. Paradoxically, however, their dependence makes them more vulnerable than the domestic sub-culture within their countries. When dealing with the sub-cultures of their own countries, the upper classes of Spanish America are under greater compulsion to be paternalistic than are foreign capitalists in their dealings with the Spanish Americans who are dependent upon them.

Economists and historians may never be able to resolve whether or not the effects of foreign capitalism have been to drain off Spanish America's economic resources without adequate compensation. Many, however, would agree that it has had a draining effect morally, by undermining the character of Spanish America's directing classes. This view, of course, implies a negative appraisal of the traditional values of the Hispanic world. The élites of Spanish America, on the other hand, find no difficulty in justifying their dependence on foreign capital. They use similar arguments to justify their dependence on the labour of serfs and peons. Like the native lower classes, foreign capitalists are regarded as incapable of adding to humanity's cultural treasure. Hence, it is considered a natural division of talent for a dominant culture to accept dependence on the manual labour of a sub-culture and on the capital of foreigners in order to liberate its members from material care and enable them to enrich the realm of the mind and spirit.

Dependence can thus be seen as strengthening rather than draining the character of the Spanish American élite, and there is no doubt that foreign capital, however unwittingly, has made a vital contribution to the preservation of Spanish America's two-culture society. Critics of the traditional society argue endlessly over who bears the major share of responsibility for its perpetuation: the foreign capitalists or the natives who have been willing to become dependent upon them. In either case, it is virtually certain that both foreign capitalists and the dominant Spanish American élite, because of their symbiotic relationship, will receive little mercy at the hands of revolutionary groups seeking to destroy the traditional social relationships.

Even without major revolutionary upheavals, a deterioration in the customary relationship between foreign capital and Spanish Americans seems likely to occur, if historical experience is any guide. In colonial times and in the period immediately following independence, the main source of monetary loans to a non-economic upper class was the Catholic Church, an institution which, in spite of its frequent denunciations of capitalist values, ran some of the most successful economic operations in Spanish America. The indebtedness of the Spanish American upper classes to the Church was endemic, but eventually they repudiated their debts and in many republics confiscated the properties and capital wealth of the Church and sought to curtail or eliminate its remaining power and temporal influence. It is hardly likely that those who replaced the Church as the principal suppliers of capital to non-economic, semi-capitalist groups will escape a similar fate.

Such conclusions can obviously only be conjectural. On the other hand, historical evidence shows clearly the tenacity of the traditional institutions and social forms. Their preservation has been achieved, as the following pages will show, in different ways in the different Spanish American republics, but it is a basic fact in the contemporary situation. Even in Mexico and Bolivia, countries which experienced successful social revolutions, the traditional two-culture society has largely been restored. Elsewhere, only since the 1950s have new challenges become clearly evident. In Cuba under Fidel Castro there emerged for the first time in Spanish American history a society radically different from the traditional one; but it is still not clear whether it will set an example or remain an exception. Developments during the first dozen years following Castro's seizure of power make the second of these possibilities seem the likelier.

12, 13 Under the presidency of General Porfirio Díaz (1830–1915), left, Mexico's *gente decente* (decent people) were encouraged in their contemptuous attitudes towards Indians and profited from government backing and connivance in the seizure of Indian communal lands. With the Revolution that began in 1910, property was in some instances restored and in others given to Indian communities that had not previously possessed it. Diego Rivera's mural, bèlow, shows land distribution in progress.

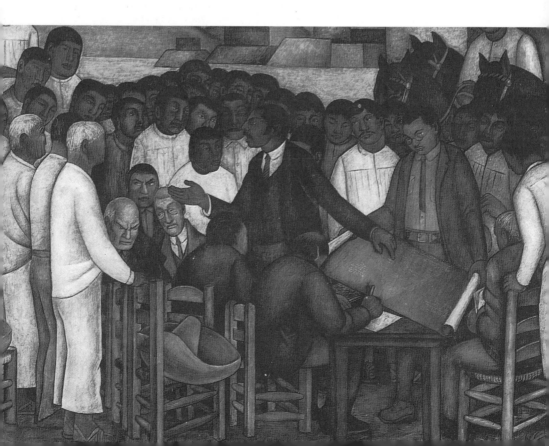

4 Social Revolution and the Traditional Society
i: The Case of Mexico

During the extended period of authoritarian rule by Porfirio Díaz – the so-called *Porfiriato* between 1876 and 1911 – racialist positivism was an important ingredient in the ideology of the Mexican governing élite. Mexico's polite society tended to regard the Indians, who constituted over 30 per cent of the country's approximately 15 million inhabitants, as innately inferior; and they talked a good deal about the need to improve the racial stock by attracting masses of white immigrants. A widespread belief in the inferiority of the Indian, accompanied by the hope that the indigenous race would ultimately disappear from the national scene beneath a wave of immigration, lay behind much of the systematic seizure of property that native communities suffered during the *Porfiriato*.

Reformist positivists challenged the assumptions of racial inferiority and averred that the Indian could be transformed. For them, Mexico's destiny lay not in immigration but in uplifting its own Indian populace. Justo Sierra, for example, one of his country's most eminent intellectuals at the turn of the century, maintained that the Indian, once properly educated, could become an instrument of national development and progress. The first volume of the important three-volume history, *México, su evolución social*, which he edited in 1900, contained a lengthy essay by a like-minded positivist, Agustín Aragón. Arguing against racialist theories, Aragón insisted that the Indian possessed an aptitude for western culture. Still, however much more kindly disposed towards the native the reformist positivists were, their ideology did not impede the despoilment of Indian communal properties, to which the racialist group was committed. In fact, those who carried out despoilment policies – in the immediate wake of which seized lands were often distributed in *minifundia* plots to individual Indians – could conveniently rationalize their actions on the grounds that they were contributing to the education of the native, helping to prepare him for western culture by forcing him to learn to function as a self-reliant private property owner.

The pressures to which, from a diversity of motives, the dominant classes subjected the Indian sub-culture caused hardship and misery and kindled anger and resentment among the country's rural poor. Against this background, alienated members of Mexico's upper groups, many of them influenced by Marxism and finding in pre-conquest Indian culture collectivist traditions which appealed enormously to them, raised the cry of revolution. The revolution they envisaged was one aimed at imposing the life style of the Indian sub-culture upon the dominant culture. These *indigenista*, or Indophile, leaders of the uprising that exploded in 1910 provided some of the goals and much of the rhetoric still associated with the Mexican Revolution. However, the Revolution was a complex phenomenon and, in addition to a disruption of the traditional relationship between the two cultures, a number of other factors helped to precipitate it.

Some of its leaders and partisans saw in the Revolution a means of spiritualizing Mexican society by cleansing the landowners and emergent bourgeoisie of their rampant materialism, while safeguarding the masses against further contamination by the germs of individualistic greed. As the instrument for spiritualizing Mexico, not a few turned towards the Catholic Church and urged the full restoration of its power and privileges, which had been seriously curtailed if not totally destroyed by the liberal governments of the 1850s and 1860s. Others, among them Antonio Caso, influenced by Rodó and the Arielist school and at least indirectly by Spanish Krausism, saw in secular humanism a means of spiritualizing the country.

Still other Mexicans of the early revolutionary period aimed primarily at greater material development, the key to which they thought, like many of the reformist positivists of the late *Porfiriato*, lay in uplifting the Indians. Because of the prevailing prejudices, they argued, during the rule of Díaz the Indian had never enjoyed a real opportunity to become acculturated into the liberal-capitalist milieu. In the Mexico of the future, racialist prejudices would be swept aside and the Indian would emerge as an effective producer and consumer within a capitalist society orientated towards material development. Many of those concerned with development desired even more in the way of government stimuli and inducements than had been furnished to the business community by dictator Díaz. Others blamed state intervention for having slowed economic progress and advocated the application of purer *laissez-faire* principles.

In addition, there were Mexicans primarily concerned with political reform. Among them was Francisco I. Madero, briefly president in the early stages of the Revolution, who apparently felt that a democratic body politic, patterned in some ways after the United States, would prove a panacea for Mexican ills. The masses, he once asserted, were more interested in the right to vote than in acquiring individual fortunes. He therefore concluded that a vast expansion of suffrage rights would provide political, and with it economic and social, stability. To many Mexicans, however, unrestricted democracy based on the principle of one man, one vote was a

14 Emiliano Zapata, who symbolized the struggle for Indian rights and agrarian reform in the Mexican Revolution; assassinated in 1919, he has since become a legendary folk-hero.

blueprint for catastrophe. Mexico, they insisted, must re-create the organic democracy of the colonial past within which people expressed themselves not as isolated individuals but rather through their corporate associations.

The attempt to describe who expected what from the Revolution could be prolonged at great length. Much more germane to the purpose of this book is to describe the system that actually emerged. It will be argued that the Revolution resulted in the rebirth of a basically two-culture society. Within this society a sub-culture, shielded against individualistic, capitalist incentives, accepted a role of dependence upon a paternalistic state; at the same time the state assisted members of the dominant culture to realize their capitalist aspirations. As a means of guaranteeing stability to the reborn two-culture society a corporative political system was established, controlled from above by a centralistic state, which permitted the masses to participate in political decision-making at the lower levels of government. A further guarantee of stability was a heady nationalism based on glorification of the Indian and his culture. In the pride and sense of dignity bestowed by the Revolution's nationalistic rhetoric, members of the sub-culture, Indians and part Indians, found non-material rewards to sustain them in their lives of subsistence and dependence.

At various times in the colonial period, though never with absolute consistency, the Spaniards pursued a policy of *dos repúblicas* (two republics). They sought, in other words, to keep the Indians, living in their accustomed manner, isolated from Spaniards who operated within an altogether different cultural ambience. Throughout the colonial period the Catholic Church laboured to impart to the members of one of the two republics a resigned acceptance of their state of temporal subsistence and dependence. In post-Revolutionary Mexico the cultural nationalism of *indigenismo*, in addition to the Catholic faith, helped to maintain a traditional society by guaranteeing the tranquil coexistence of the *dos repúblicas*, of the two cultures.

A symbol of the achievements of post-Revolutionary Mexico on the social-political level is provided by the country's outstanding historian of ideas, Leopoldo Zea. He interprets Mexican history as a progressive effort at emancipation from the institutions, society, and especially from the values, of the Spanish colonial régime. Yet, Zea is also seeking for Mexico's cultural peculiarity, its unique national essence. And the deeper he probes for the essence of Mexico's national identity, the more he tends to be driven back towards the values and life styles associated with the former *madre patria*.

Much the same is true of the Mexican Revolution. In the attempt to escape foreign influences and to forge a new Mexico through revolution, Mexicans have come back to a social structure that has many of its roots in their Hispanic background. Although often pictured as a wildly innovating revolutionary, Lázaro Cárdenas was the principal guiding spirit of this return to traditionalism in Mexico. It was during his presidential term (1934–40) that Mexicans developed or improved most of the formulae and institutional machinery needed to re-establish a harmonious relationship between its two internal cultures, the dominant and the subordinate.

Under Cárdenas the corporative apparatus of the country's official party (the Partido de la Revolución Mexicana, rechristened the Partido Revolucionario Institucional in 1946), the only party generally permitted to win elections, was perfected. As reorganized by Cárdenas the official party had four sectors: agriculture, labour, military and popular, the last a catch-all category whose main component was the government bureaucracy and into which the military was later incorporated. In the popular sector were also included certain non-industrial unions, organizations of professional men, youth groups, co-operative societies and a number of miscellaneous associations. Because of the corporative nature of the official party, the faithful participated within it less as individuals than as members of a particular functional group. Society was compartmentalized, the members of each compartment at the grass roots selecting individuals who served at the next highest level in a vertical, hierarchical structure. This procedure, with its built-in screening devices, provided a safeguard against the allegedly levelling effects of egalitarian, one man, one vote democracy, which the political thinkers of the Spanish-speaking world have consistently rejected. At the highest level, the national party exercised a moderating power among the various corporative entities comprising it. So long as members of each corporation were persuaded that their interests were adequately protected, they remained willing to recognize the legitimacy of the party's top echelon and to accept decisions handed down by it in the exercise of its moderating power.

The dependence of the labour unions – the major element within the labour sector – upon the government provided an additional assurance of the smooth functioning of the corporative structure in Mexico. Union leaders, whose organizations lacked the power and independence to pose a direct challenge to the management-ownership sector, secured benefits for their rank and file by bargaining with government. Under Cárdenas, moreover, the advantages won by organized labour as often as not took the form of fringe benefits. Certainly, between 1936 and 1938 real wages declined sharply. Furthermore, steady inflation discouraged savings, leaving the workers all the more dependent upon a paternalistic government.

A penetrating analysis of the Spanish American situation made by Ronald C. Newton in 1970 is strikingly applicable to Mexico under Cárdenas. According to Newton, the free professions are not really free.

Doctors, lawyers and other professional men have been organized into associations that are intimately dependent upon the government, both for employment and for the enjoyment of the privileges ensured by the more or less complete monopoly of the national universities in granting degrees and licences to practise. Newton points out that these interest groups are remarkably similar to the corporative associations of the *ancien régime*, and suggests that they may indicate the revival of a system assumed to have passed into oblivion with the disintegration of Spain's American empire.

If, under Cárdenas, the members of the free professions, men of some prominence in the dominant culture, received concessions and favours that assured their loyalty to the established system and at the same time reduced them to relative dependence, the status of dependence was far more pronounced in the case of the urban working classes. Even more pronounced was the dependence of the largest element of the sub-culture, the predominantly Indian rural labourers.

Cárdenas carried out a massive programme of land redistribution that, temporarily at least, wiped out the old *haciendas* and the existing pattern of large-scale private landownership in much of Mexico. By 1945, largely as a result of processes set in motion by Cárdenas, land had been given to over 20,000 Indian communities, referred to as *ejidos*. In some instances, use of the land was assigned to individual families, the ideal being that each family should receive 4·6 hectares (there are 2·47 acres in a hectare). However, on some of the largest *ejidos* land was not parcelled out individually to the community-dwellers or *ejidatarios*; instead, it was owned and worked collectively, and the profits realized from the sale of produce were shared collectively. Through the distribution of land to *ejidos*, a semi-communal system, reminiscent of the corporative patterns of colonial times, came into being.

Critics of the system maintained, with some justification, that the *ejidatarios* – who in 1940 constituted about 50 per cent of the agricultural population and made up the bulk of the official party's agricultural sector – had merely changed masters. Instead of being dependent upon the private landowner or *hacendado*, they had become dependent upon the central government that controlled credit facilities, frequently determined what crops were to be planted, and in general exercised an overweening influence in all spheres of *ejidal* life. That *ejidatarios* became dependent is scarcely surprising. Cárdenas, a bulwark of traditionalism, would scarcely have desired to encourage competitiveness, independence and self-reliance among men who made up a good percentage of the sub-culture.

In maintaining the dependence of the sub-culture and in isolating its members from the values of an individualistic, acquisitive capitalist world, Cárdenas relied also on the socialist tone that came to characterize primary

15, 16 Two Mexican presidents. Above, the visionary and pliable Francisco I. Madero riding into Mexico City; his ineffective administration, characterized by concern with political democracy rather than social and economic reform, ended with his assassination in 1913. Right, the idealistic but also shrewd, pragmatic and tough Lázaro Cárdenas: extensive land redistribution, the nationalization of foreign oil concerns and the strengthening of corporative political devices were among the notable features of his term of office (1934–40).

instruction in the public school system – significantly the university system, more the province of the dominant culture, rejected a socialist orientation. The president also relied on an emotional rhetoric of nationalism that glorified the collective Indian heritage. However, the Indian glorified by Mexican nationalism came, during the rule of Cárdenas, to be not the pre-conquest native but instead the Hispanicized, Catholicized Indian. Impressed by the gains scored among the Indians of central Mexico by an anti-government, rabidly pro-Catholic movement known as *sinarquismo*, the essentially pragmatic Cárdenas took action to pacify his Catholic critics. In late 1936 the president began to seek an understanding with the Church. From that time the Revolution was no longer associated, as it had been by many of its early leaders, including perhaps Cárdenas himself when he was younger, with an attempt to extirpate Catholicism from Mexican soil. Instead of trying to destroy the Church, Cárdenas came to accept it as a useful ally – although one that had to be kept at arm's length because of the Revolution's continuing anti-clerical image, which served an important function in maintaining the allegiance of many intellectuals – in spreading among the working classes a non-materialistic set of values that equated resigned acceptance of dependence and poverty in this life with Christian virtue.

In resorting to collectivism as one of several elements, including Catholicism, in a national policy aimed at retaining a rural sub-culture in its traditional non-capitalist mode of existence and at assuring a harmonious relationship between the rural workers and the dominant élite, Cárdenas came close – unwittingly, apparently, rather than by design – to implementing a programme formulated in the late nineteenth century by the Spaniard Joaquín Costa. An intellectual who was to acquire widespread prominence throughout the Hispanic world, particularly after his death in 1911, Costa had urged the restoration of social harmony to a dangerously divided Spain by means of a collectivized rural economy to be achieved by the return of communal properties to villages. Discontent in the country-side had been caused, he believed, by the seizure, beginning in 1837, of communal properties, prompted in part by a misguided attempt to convert peasants to liberalism by turning them into private landowners. At the same time, Costa also favoured policies to encourage the rise of an urban bourgeoisie dedicated to the capitalist values of individual economic aggrandizement. According to him, only a capitalist bourgeoisie could achieve the economic development upon which Spain's future depended. But the peasantry would inevitably disrupt the operation of bourgeois capitalism unless afforded security within a collectivized rural economy assumed to be in keeping with its natural preferences and inclinations.

Not only did Cárdenas try to re-establish Mexico's traditional semi-collectivist rural economy; he also – in a way that Costa would have approved – provided inducements and rewards to a development-minded, thoroughly materialistic bourgeoisie. Although the highest accolades accorded him often come from Marxists and left-wing intellectuals, Lázaro Cárdenas actually laid the foundation for the economic development which has benefited a bourgeois plutocracy. As Albert L. Michaels wrote in 1970, 'Many observers do not realize the impetus that the Cárdenas government gave to private industry. . . . The government sought to divert Mexican capital, which formerly went into the land, into domestic development. . . . His vast public works programs and the Nacional Financiera [the official development bank] had been designed to bolster, not destroy capitalism.'

The genius of the controversial Mexican president lay in his ability to devise a reasonably balanced programme of concessions. Favours were distributed fairly equitably among the various groups of the sub-culture and among the new capitalist members of the dominant culture who, by the end of the 1930s, were already contributing more than public institutions to the economic development that was soon to become a source of untold national pride. Succeeding administrations, on the other hand, have tended to reserve favours to a considerable extent for the industrial-entrepreneurial élite. This has resulted in an abiding and perhaps deepening social problem. However, another result of post-Cárdenas policies, as Professor Frank Brandenburg pointed out in 1964, was that capitalists who might otherwise have contributed vigorously to a dissenting right-wing nationalism lent loyal support to the established system.

The development of Mexico had its psychological as well as its economic aspect. Prior to the Revolution, the economic élite had been largely dependent and subservient in its dealings with foreign capital. From the early days of the Revolution, the attitude of the bourgeoisie changed. It began to cast off its sense of inferiority and summon up the confidence needed to end its reliance on the foreigners who had controlled much of the Mexican economy. It took control of the economy and eventually, as it gained faith in its economic abilities, it welcomed foreign capitalists back to the land, but this time more as partners than masters.

The emotional high-point in the quest for greater economic independence came in 1938, when Cárdenas nationalized foreign oil holdings. This dramatic act, preceded by many years of less spectacular but equally important assertions of economic nationalism as Mexican capitalists privately struggled towards greater independence, was skilfully utilized by Cárdenas as a means of exhorting the working classes to greater efforts. After the expropriation, the president called upon workers to show their patriotism by assuming new sacrifices and developing greater efficiency so as to consolidate economic independence. In equating patriotism with increased productivity, Cárdenas obviously hoped to bring about a situation in which more would come from the workers; on the other hand, much of what went to the workers would be intangible satisfaction attendant upon pride in contributing to national progress. In so far as he was successful in this approach, the president had hit upon a way to stimulate the productivity of workers without arousing unduly their desire for individual economic betterment and power.

Since the 1940s it has become increasingly clear that the Mexican workers have received primarily intangible gratifications as their share in the Revolution's rewards. Meanwhile, many of those in the upper groups of Mexican society have grown rich and powerful in a process that has produced one of the most successful capitalist groups in Spanish America's history. Beginning in the mid-1950s Mexico's annual growth rate reached an impressive and long sustained figure of between 6 and 7 per cent; and per capita gross national product, despite an annual population increase of close to 4 per cent, doubled between 1950 and 1970. The material benefits of this remarkable development, however, were shared by only a quarter, or at best one-third, of the population. Judged by economic indices, the rest of the population is no better off, and may even be slightly worse off, than before the Revolution began in 1910.

In spite of this, comparative data assembled by Gabriel Almond and Sidney Verba in 1963 suggest that in the late 1950s and early 1960s the Mexican political and economic system enjoyed a relatively high degree of acceptance. Among the statistics collected by them, based on widespread responses to questionnaires and interviews, the following are particularly pertinent to the present study.

Country	Percentage of respondents who could name at least four national leaders of principal parties	Percentage who could name no such leaders	Percentage proud of government and political institutions	Percentage proud of economic system
United States	65	16	85	23
Great Britain	42	20	46	10
Germany	69	12	7	33
Italy	36	40	3	3
Mexico	5	53	30	24

These figures indicate that a fairly high percentage of Mexicans were proud of the country's government and political institutions, even though they could not name four national leaders of political parties. Perhaps this points to the validity of assumptions commonly made by advocates of the corporative structure. If people are content with political activity at a subsidiary level in minor groups and associations, they will be little concerned about policies and leaders at the top or national level.

These statistics may indicate that people may remain content with an economic system that denies them material rewards and self-reliance, provided that system bestows non-material gratifications. Perhaps the miracle of modern Mexico is not the economic development achieved by a new plutocracy within the dominant culture so much as the degree to which the members of the sub-culture have remained willing to eschew the values associated with economic independence and to settle for moral rewards and for security within an existence of subsistence level. This possibility may seem strange to foreign observers who are the products of societies in which bourgeois, capitalist incentives have permeated all classes; but it may explain the way in which, following a violent social revolution, Mexicans have gradually reverted to a semi-traditional two-culture society.

If Mexico's post-Revolutionary society must be described as semi-traditional, it is because the dominant culture has largely absorbed and accepted bourgeois standards. The non-capitalist and even anti-capitalist values that were characteristic of aristocratic society in the Hispanic world have become rare and difficult to detect, although they still exist among certain intellectual and professional groups, and even businessmen pay lip service to them.

In one of his most celebrated books Oscar Lewis produced testimony that the children of Sánchez, with the sole exception of Consuelo, were resigned to their poverty, did not feel unjustly discriminated against or unduly deprived, and were largely unmotivated by ambitions to rise in social status. Evidently there are many others like the children of Sánchez in Mexico's sub-culture, its culture of poverty.

In recent years, however, new social pressures and serious divisions have begun to appear in Mexico. The collectivist farming structure that Cárdenas viewed as a means of bringing satisfaction and security to the peasant class has largely broken down. Moreover, Mexico's burgeoning population, amounting in 1970 to approximately 48 million people, 19 million of whom are under twelve years of age, is placing increasing pressures upon the government's social services. Indications abound that Mexico's plutocracy, made ever more greedy by success, is becoming less and less willing to contribute the money that is needed to meet the demands of social services. In their present mood the nation's economic titans may be repeating the fatal mistake made by those of the *Porfiriato*; for they appear to be adopting a liberal, *laissez-faire* approach to economics when the masses are not competent to shift for themselves within a liberal economic structure and when

53

17 Student poster demanding freedom of expression displayed during the 1968 Olympic Games in Mexico: an estimated two hundred people were killed in clashes between soldiers and students during the Games.

the whole socio-economic and political system is geared to preventing them from acquiring such competence.

In the 1950s Mexican intellectuals increasingly began to condemn conditions within their country, lamenting that the Revolution was dead. Criticism did not necessarily spring from a desire to see the lot of the lower classes fundamentally altered. Certainly a good number even of those who are most outspokenly critical of Mexican socio-economic conditions accept it as natural for the masses to remain dependent. Many of the bitterest critics of contemporary Mexico object, as humanists, to the materialism of a bourgeoisie that seems to be establishing the patterns of national character among the dominant culture. Persuaded that Mexico must always seek its true identity in humanist values, intellectuals alienated by many features of the prevailing system charge a rapacious group of business leaders with having sold out the genuine national heritage by accepting foreign cultural criteria, particularly those of the United States. Perhaps the intellectuals who censure the business élite worry that if the masses are not set an example from the social world above them, save that of the mad pursuit of wealth, they too will eventually acquire habits of unbridled materialism, thus destroying the balance between the two cultures and jeopardizing the traditional society.

Whether or not its leaders can carry out the reforms called for in the interest of self-preservation, it remains true that the Mexican system, as it developed after the Revolution of 1910, restored the viability of the traditional society and sustained many aspects of it for over half a century. Revolution was necessary because the country's leaders during the *Porfiriato* had consciously discarded most of the devices and attitudes developed during the colonial period, upon which the maintenance of the two-culture structure depended. The new Mexican leaders did not, in most instances, intend to return to the old and traditional social forms; generally, in fact, they rejected them and had never directly experienced them. But somehow the lingering influence of a cultural environment that had originated mainly in the southern and central Iberian peninsula led them back subconsciously – in a process that science cannot adequately explain – to what was traditional, thereby permitting them once more to be original, by being themselves.

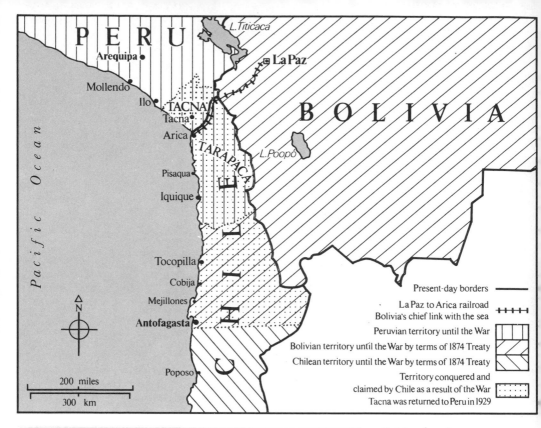

PERU

Arequipa •

Mollendo •

Ilo •
TACNA
Tacna •

Arica •

L. Titicaca

La Paz

BOLIVIA

TARAPACA

L. Poopó

Pisagua •

Iquique •

C H I L E

Tocopilla •

Cobija •

Mejillones •

Antofagasta •

Poposo •

Pacific Ocean

200 miles

300 km

Present-day borders ——————
La Paz to Arica railroad
Bolivia's chief link with the sea ✛✛✛✛✛
Peruvian territory until the War
Bolivian territory until the War by terms of 1874 Treaty
Chilean territory until the War by terms of 1874 Treaty
Territory conquered and claimed by Chile as a result of the War
Tacna was returned to Peru in 1929

18 Map showing the areas disputed during the War of the Pacific (1879–83).

19 A Quechua Indian village in Bolivia's highland plateau.

5 Social Revolution and the Traditional Society
ii: The Case of Bolivia

Bolivia, another Spanish American republic with a large Indian population, was by the mid-twentieth century confronting a revolutionary situation. Circumstances different from, although in some respects analogous to, those in Mexico made it necessary for Bolivia to undergo a revolution in order to salvage many of the most distinctive features of its historic way of life.

Crushingly defeated by Chile and deprived of its coastal territory in the west, Bolivia had emerged from the War of the Pacific (1879–83) a land-locked republic. Concentrated in the *altiplano* (highland plateau), between one-half and two-thirds of its population of considerably under 2 million consisted principally of unassimilated Aymara and Quechua Indians. Most of the remaining Bolivians were *cholos* (in this republic a term for Euro-peanized Indians) or mestizos (mixed bloods). A tiny minority claiming pure Spanish ancestry made up much of the top social, political and economic élites.

In 1900 between 70 and 80 per cent of the population was rural, and no great influx into the cities was yet under way. A considerable proportion of the Indians, making up the bulk of the rural population, still lived in *comuni-dades*, dating back to the Spanish colonial period, where land was held in common. The *comunidades* claimed about one-twentieth of the land in the *altiplano*. Many other Indians lived as vassals (*colonos*) on the *latifundia* owned privately by some of the country's most illustrious families. Indians dwelling in *comunidades* generally managed to eke out a subsistence existence and, fearing that any innovation might produce adverse effects and drive them below the subsistence level, maintained staunchly conservative attitudes. Indians ensnared as vassals, although their lives could be bleak and trying, were often maintained at something above bare subsistence standards by various paternalistic devices initiated during the colonial period.

On the whole, rural Bolivia was quiescent, largely because the masses were left alone and not subjected to demands that they reform themselves. The explanation for this lies partly in the widespread conviction among the country's accommodated groups that Indians were innately inferior, a 'hopeless race'. Typical exponents of the pervasive pessimism of the Bolivian upper classes about the potential of the Indians were the historian Gabriel René-Moreno and the pseudo sociologist-historian Alcides Argüedas. In his best known work, *Pueblo enfermo* (1909), Argüedas maintained that the Bolivian masses were a sick people, psychologically and physically. Whether or not he felt there was any hope that they might emerge from their sickness is still debated by the country's intellectuals.

Unlike the racialists of Mexico, who looked to immigration to improve the nation, their ideological counterparts in Bolivia accepted the fact that relatively few immigrants could be lured to their land. Accordingly, they resigned themselves to leaving their Indians, the only labour force available to them, largely alone. They also refrained from systematic attempts to hasten the Indian's disappearance, through such expedients as seizure of communal property, in expectation of the arrival of a superior labour force.

Other sections of the upper classes lined up with Jaime Mendoza in their attitudes towards the Indian. Mendoza, a medical doctor with a special interest in psychology, and also a poet, explorer, geographer, novelist and historian, believed it possible that the Indian might be endowed with vitality and a high potential; but he was by no means certain. He sought, therefore, to study the Indian scientifically, something until then scarcely attempted in Bolivia. Whatever potential the Indian might have, Mendoza affirmed, should be developed within his own way of life. He did not want to Europeanize the native, but rather to conserve him as an autochthonous man. Essentially, Mendoza harked back to the Spanish colonial approach of segregation or *dos repúblicas*: one republic for Indians, another for the non-Indian population.

Whether Bolivians professed the innate inferiority of Indians or believed that the potential of the natives could best be realized in a separate existence, the overall social consequences of their convictions were likely to be the same. In neither case would there be a sustained effort by the dominant culture to intrude upon or to try to change and reform the Indian subculture.

Many Bolivians doubted the capacity not only of Indians but of mestizos as well. The widespread pessimism among Bolivians about the potential of their 'race' fostered a do-nothing attitude that was not conducive to the growth of revolutionary activity. No matter how disaffected they are with the existing order, revolutionaries will hesitate to take to the barricades in the attempt to topple it unless they hope that the people whom they propose to lead are capable of responding to their dreams for a better society.

Taking advantage of the prevailing calm in rural Bolivia, and perhaps chastened by humiliating military defeat into assuming a more responsible attitude, the country's leaders managed, after the War of the Pacific, to achieve a higher degree of political stability than had previously obtained. A constitution enacted in 1880 remained in effect until 1938. Under it the Conservative Party dominated the country's politics until 1899, when the Liberals came to power. Leaders of both political pressure groups – they were not true parties – tended to avoid ideological intransigence and maintained a dialogue of co-operation with each other in encouraging railroad-building and the development of modern mining enterprises. A Republican Party, founded in 1915 and coming to power five years later under Bautista Saavedra, continued the patterns of government established by Conservatives and Liberals. The Republicans also made some half-hearted attempts to introduce a government-controlled programme of paternalism by enacting the country's first social welfare legislation.

By the turn of the century mining had become a principal base of the Bolivian economy. By the end of the 1920s Bolivia was producing annually nearly 30 per cent of the world's supply of tin. Political control was exercised by the notorious *rosca*, an interlocking directorate of economic interests made up in part of landowners but dominated by tin magnates such as the Patiños, Aramayos and Hocschilds. In its lower echelons the *rosca* included a host of lawyers, bureaucrats and politicians who served the interests of the Bolivian lords of tin and also of the foreign firms and the international cartels on which these magnates were to a considerable extent dependent. Colourful and highly critical accounts of the *rosca* and its manipulations are found in works by Augusto Céspedes and Sergio Almaraz that have been widely influential among literate Bolivians.

In the 1920s and 1930s an increasing number of middle-sector political figures and *pensadores* grew incensed at the corrupt practices of the power-mad *rosca*, which was siphoning off national wealth for the benefit of a tiny handful of Bolivians and a few foreigners and in the process subjecting thousands of Indian and *cholo* miners to inhuman labour conditions. Outraged by this situation and insisting upon sweeping change, alienated intellectuals began to challenge the once widely accepted belief in the racial inferiority of the vast masses of Bolivians. One of them, Carlos Medinaceli, praised the mestizo, picturing him as combining the best features of the two civilizations, Indian and Spanish, that had produced him. Far more assertive and vociferous were the *indigenistas* who ascribed virtue and capacity almost exclusively to the Indian.

Gustavo Adolfo Navarro (pseudonym Tristán Marof) saw a golden age in the Indian past, attributing all the country's ills to the greed and vice introduced by the Spanish *conquistadores*. He alleged that the country was being bled by a corrupt alliance of intellectuals, lawyers, military officers and priests, all of them the sycophantic allies of an *oligarquía* of *criollos* that had sold out the country to foreign interests. An even more extreme pro-

Indian racist who fulminated against all those who had a drop of European blood was Franz Tamayo. For him, Bolivian history from the time of the conquest was without redeeming feature, for it was only the story of perverse and debased Spaniards and of psychologically demented *cholos* and mestizos who were corrupted by Spanish culture and blood.

At the same time a group of more conservative intellectuals, led by Roberto Prudencio among others, made harsh criticisms of many features of contemporary Bolivian life. Their analysis, however, did not see the pre-conquest era as a model for an ideal, socialist Bolivia of the future. Prudencio and his intellectual companions found much to admire in the colonial period, when the Indian allegedly had benefited from the paternalistic protection of Spanish administrators and landowners. The Indian, they agreed, possessed potential and capacity, but in his Hispanicized form, moulded and shaped by the paternal institutions of Church and state. Bolivia had been betrayed not by the Spaniards and their traditions of the colonial period, but by the money-mad *nouveaux riches* elements which had grasped at the alien ideologies of liberalism and positivism in order to rationalize their greed. While Marxists might be justified in their denunciation of the present order, they were said to be mistaken in turning to yet another foreign ideology as the solution.

The mounting tide of intellectual criticism gave rise to a wide variety of political action groups. On the left there appeared, among many others, the Grupo Túpac Amaru, advocating violent overthrow of the government, nationalization of the tin mines and collectivization of the entire agrarian sector; the Grupo de Izquierda, a Marxist association with headquarters in Cochabamba; and the Partido Izquierda Revolucionario, a Trotskyite organization. Closer to the centre were various political groups that urged the total socialization of the country's economy through peaceful, evolutionary means. Squarely in the centre stood those critics of the existing régime who advocated remedies based on slightly greater government intervention in the social and economic spheres. On the right a variety of associations surfaced, some led by military officers, others by intellectuals who turned for inspiration to Catholic social philosophy, which urged the formation of a corporative state so as to have done with the farce of liberal, parliamentary democracy. The military groups, on the whole, desired a highly centralized corporative structure, one within which economic development could be sought through authoritarian means. The Catholic associations, on the other hand, tended to minimize the importance of economic development and to censure materialistic incentives. At the same time they championed a decentralized structure within which diverse regional and functional groups would be largely free from state control but scrupulously attentive to directives from the episcopacy.

Ideological fragmentation, reflected in the political arena by a plethora of new pressure groups grandiloquently termed parties by their members, produced a modern variant of the corporative state. In the traditional corporative state each person was to realize himself and play his part in society by participating within a functional or municipal or regional group that was appropriate, natural and convenient to him. Within the ideological and political maze that Bolivia was becoming in the 1920s and 1930s, each person was able to identify himself with and participate in an ideological and/or political splinter group that reflected very closely his own highly personal set of interests, incentives and moral judgments. Probably the vast majority of those associated with these groups did not expect their particular organization to acquire any sizable share of power. But the mere existence of these groups afforded members a congenial place in society and a means for deriving a feeling of dignity and a sense of belonging by joining with and being heeded by like-minded individuals. Government fulfilled the role expected of it not by surrendering its powers to any one of the numerous groups, but simply by permitting the continued existence of all of them and by occasionally adopting some of their pet policies. With this arrangement, no one had to compromise his basic tenets, as would have been the case in a mass party. In return for not having to compromise his more cherished ideas and ideals, in return for not having to moderate his voice as he spoke within the confines of his own peer group, the individual accepted a situation in which the collective voice of his group might be a scarcely audible chorus in a huge and complex symphony made up of innumerable choirs.

In any corporative structure, harmony and order depend ultimately on the ability of government, through the exercise of a moderating power, to resolve disputes among the corporations and to fuse the divergent and sometimes mutually exclusive policies and aspirations of each into some sort of a cohesive whole. No administration, however, can exercise a moderating power unless its authority as an ultimate arbiter is accepted by a significant percentage of the corporative entities and their members. In short, no government can exercise a moderating power unless it enjoys legitimacy. And, in Spanish America, with its traditional two-culture society, governmental legitimacy disappears when a majority of middle sectors, of those who are on the fringes of power within the dominant culture, ceases to identify itself with an upper-class élite that basically controls the machinery of government. When middle sectors within the dominant culture no longer serve as guardians of an upper-class world which they themselves aspire to enter, and set out instead to destroy that world, a revolutionary situation is at hand.

In the late 1930s Bolivia had entered upon a revolutionary situation, in part because of the consequences of the Chaco War (1932–35). In 1932 President Daniel Salamanca, leader of one wing of a split Republican Party and a symbol of the old-guard power clique that had controlled politics through the *rosca*, took advantage of a complex set of circumstances that had produced mounting tensions with Paraguay to precipitate a war with the neighbouring republic. Through the war he hoped to recoup his sagging political fortunes by posing as a defender of national interests. Salamanca failed ignominiously in his scheme. As several members of the president's general staff had predicted, the war ended in disaster for Bolivia. Blaming the clique that had long dominated the political scene for having started the war and for then having colossally mismanaged it, men who had previously been content to remain on the periphery of power and to serve the interests of the *rosca* began to think of overthrowing those above them.

20, 21 The Chaco War (1932–35), for Bolivia – favoured by Chile – an attempt at self-aggrandizement, for Paraguay – urged on by Argentina – a struggle to retain long-disputed territory judged essential to national survival, resulted in victory for Paraguay after three years' hard fighting on bleak and barren terrain. Left, Bolivian troops march through La Paz; right, a Paraguayan soldier.

In the aftermath of the Chaco War the masses showed signs of increasing restlessness. Many Indian conscripts into the Bolivian army, now that they had been given some of the rudiments of a primary education and afforded a new vision of their country and their position in it by being uprooted and forced out of the confines of their native localities, proved reluctant to revert to their old style of life once the war ended. In addition, an expanding urban labour force grew discontented as wages failed to keep pace with a cost of living index that rose some 217 per cent between 1931 and 1936. During the war, moreover, the government had had to retrench on the meagre investments that it had begun to make in social services under the Saavedra administration of the 1920s.

A crisis was at hand. But the situation had not yet become hopeless for the *rosca*'s leaders. They survived, although with their powers considerably curtailed, under the military régimes of David Toro and Germán Busch, which between 1936 and 1939 manipulated with at least a modicum of ability the diverse political and ideological splinter groups and pursued interventionist policies that mitigated a few of the symptoms of social malaise. Coming to the presidency in late 1943, Gualberto Villarroel ruled in heavy-handed manner but did share some political power with the Movimiento Nacionalista Revolucionario (MNR), a party founded in 1941 that ran the ideological gamut from Marxism to conservative corporativism and that depended for support largely upon the middle sectors of society. This was the first party in Bolivian history to acquire a mass following, and Víctor Paz Estenssoro, one of its leaders, served as finance minister under Villarroel. Hoping to calm the rising tide of discontent, the

22 Dwarfed by an enormous poster of himself, President Paz Estenssoro greets his followers: unable to harness the forces Bolivia's social revolution had set loose, Paz's rule became increasingly authoritarian, until he was finally overthrown by the military in 1964.

new finance minister began to augment investment in social services, even though this appreciably diminished the public funds available for economic development.

Then, in July 1946, after two and a half years in power, Villarroel was ousted from the presidency and shortly afterwards lynched by a frenzied mob, whereupon many of the important MNR leaders fled into exile. Once again wielding nearly complete but extremely precarious power, the beleaguered *oligarquía* ignored the pleas of Bautista Saavedra to expand dramatically government social service programmes and to open their ranks and share political control with elements of the disaffected middle sectors. Had they followed this advice, the *oligarquía* might still have saved themselves. Instead, they abandoned many of the social programmes timorously introduced in the past. At the same time, rather than seeking accommodation with the many groups on the lower rungs of the political ladder, and rather than trying to manipulate and to balance the multitude of pressure groups, the old guard closed its ranks against newcomers, indiscriminately repressed political associations, and sought to strengthen its grip on power through agreements with the military. In this process it lost the last vestige of legitimacy.

Out of this situation came a violent upheaval, bringing the MNR under Paz Estenssoro to power in 1952. Friend and foe alike were soon describing the upheaval as a social revolution. The revolution resulted in a drastic change in the composition of the governing élite. It produced further signicant, even profound, changes. However, whether it fundamentally altered the nature of a traditional, essentially two-culture society is a matter that remains in doubt. There is much evidence that it did not.

In one of its first acts the revolutionary government nationalized the major tin mines owned by the hated symbols of *vendepatrias* (those who sell out their countries to foreigners), the Patiños, the Aramayos and the Hoc-schilds. Labourers employed in the nationalized mines were called upon to make sacrifices in order to consolidate the country's economic independence in much the same terms that Lázaro Cárdenas had used in appealing to Mexican workers after the 1938 petroleum expropriation. Beyond nationalistic oratory, however, the government took few, if any, steps to prod workers into augmented productivity. On the contrary, feather-bedding practices were encouraged and workers were generally pampered with an uncommon array of fringe benefits. Between 1952 and 1962 production in the nationalized mines registered a decline estimated by some economists at 40 per cent. Nevertheless, the government's policies, however questionable on economic grounds, contributed to social stability. A powerful element of the labour force was won over to the new administration as the government sought to make that element dependent upon it. Bolivia's

MNR régime, however, was unable to complete this aspect of its revolution, and there remained some question as to whether the tin miners were dependent upon the government or the government upon them. The attempt to establish dependence through persuasion and the carrot having failed, the military, seizing power in 1964, resorted more to coercion and the stick in establishing the dependence of the miners.

There is sharp disagreement whether the new men who came to power after the 1952 revolution voluntarily initiated land reform, or whether it was forced upon a reluctant administration by aroused Indian masses, sometimes in collaboration with extreme leftist elements within the loosely disciplined and perennially divided MNR. Apparently the situation varied a great deal from region to region, with some Indian communities demonstrating militancy while others simply awaited and then accepted government actions in a spirit of docility. Whatever the circumstances, there is no question that in the years between 1952 and 1956 Bolivia underwent the most massive change in landownership that Spanish America had witnessed since the days of Cárdenas in Mexico. In the process a large portion of Bolivia's landowning élite was eliminated. Virtually all land seized from its former owners was redistributed on the basis of fee-simple ownership. Recent studies by anthropologists and sociologists have established that communal-collectivist traditions had largely disappeared among both the Quechua and Aymara Indians of Bolivia prior to the revolution. What the Indians wanted – if indeed they desired change at all – was private ownership, especially of the small plots of land they had previously held in usufruct in compensation for the labour they performed for the owners of large estates. And, it was private property that the Indians gained through the revolution. Thus there came into being, for the first time in the country's history, a numerically significant class of landowning peasants. Preliminary indications suggest that the new Bolivian peasantry may, on the whole, be as conservative as were the peasants of France and northern Spain during most of the past century and a half. This, at least, is one of the meanings that some observers draw from the failure of 'Che' Guevara to evoke an enthusiastic response from the newly established peasant groups in whose midst he operated in 1967.

Satisfaction for peasants in post-revolutionary Bolivia derives not only from the ownership of property but also from liberation from former conditions of vassalage that forced them in many parts of the country to work three and even four days a week for the owner of a large estate in return for the use of a miniscule plot of land. Satisfaction derives also from the fact that the revolutionary government has lacked the means to intrude consistently into the newly independent world of the Indian peasants so as to enforce rational investment of income and efficient methods of agricultural production. The peasants on the whole have remained free to invest their income economically or to squander it in conspicuous consumption during fiestas. In addition, they have remained free to farm efficiently or to use their land simply to assure a subsistence existence. If they opted for subsistence, they could still experience a sense of dignity, for subsistence was no longer associated with vassalage.

Through their associations (known as *sindicatos*) Bolivia's post-revolutionary peasants have been able to share in numerous decisions that most immediately affect them, to establish schools and clinics, and to distribute the meagre funds that government has made available for agrarian reform. Through their *sindicatos* they also select men – or bestow acceptance on those who usurp the function – to represent them in the outside, non-peasant world. In the early days of the revolution, the government – just as in its dealings with the tin miners of the nationalized operations – lacked effective means for disciplining and co-ordinating the activities of Indian *sindicatos*. The situation was so chaotic as to border on anarchy, and this fact was seized upon by the military as justification for their 1964 *coup*. As the 1970s began, it was still impossible to know if the officers would attempt to further the assimilation of the Indians into the rest of Bolivian society, or

23 Women queue outside a state-owned store at a Bolivian tin mine: a significant consequence of the 1952 revolution was the nationalization of the three largest tin-mining enterprises.

24 Effigy to 'Teo', the earth-spirit, erected by Bolivian miners, evidence of the strength of traditional Indian culture in a society into which Christianity was introduced more than four centuries ago.

whether they would allow the Indians to retain what traditionally has been most precious to many of them: freedom from the intrusion of alien forces.

Most of Bolivia's peasants were Indians. But Indian had become a term of opprobrium, not unlike 'Nigger' in the United States. After the revolution the word was officially banished from the Bolivian vocabulary. Henceforth, Bolivia's rural labourers were to be referred to only as *campesinos*. With the suppression of the word Indian, there also disappeared the various legal restrictions once applied to Indians. And, as this was accomplished, the government fostered a new rhetoric of nationalism that paid homage to the non-acquisitive, stoic virtues of the selfless peasant and pictured him as the worthiest of all Bolivians. This too contributed to the pride and sense of dignity of peasants.

In dealing with urban labourers, the MNR government fashioned lavish new programmes of paternalism which, if they vastly increased the security of the masses, at the same time assured their dependence. A wide cross-section of workers, organized into government-controlled unions, soon came to share with the tin miners' union a previously undreamt of set of social and economic benefits. As Bolivia's revolutionary president, Paz Estenssoro secured much of the money required to finance the government's social programmes from the aid that the United States funnelled into Bolivia during the Eisenhower administration (1953–61) in the fear that the country might otherwise veer to the left and fall under Communist control.

In his study *The Bolivian Revolution and U.S. Aid Since 1952* (1969), Professor James W. Wilkie estimates that up to the end of 1964 only 18 per cent of the funds Bolivia received from the United States went into economic development. Most of the rest helped finance the new paternalism. In this respect, revolutionary Bolivia was not much different from the conservatively administered Spanish American republics of the 1920s which relied upon foreign sources to fund programmes aimed at restoring social peace. One difference was that in the 1920s the money derived largely from imposts on foreign enterprises and from private loans, while in revolutionary Bolivia it came directly from the United States government and public lending agencies in the form of loans, grants and concealed grants.

In revolutionary Bolivia, as in revolutionary Mexico, steps were taken to facilitate the growth of a new capitalist élite at the same time as the quiescence of the masses was assured through social services and other paternalistic devices. While tin production in the nationalized mines declined drastically between 1952 and 1962, the privately owned mines tripled their production of the metal. (Bolivian statistics must be treated with caution, for in the mid-1960s even so fundamental a point as whether the population was 3·8 or 4·4 million was disputed.) In the process some new fortunes were made and some old ones enhanced. And, while production of the crops affected by land reform, especially potatoes, corn and wheat, declined, necessitating expensive measures to import food, output – especially of rice and sugar – on non-reformed, privately owned estates (some of which belonged to Japanese immigrants attracted through government colonization projects) soared dramatically. Moreover, at least until 1956, when, as a result of United States prodding, Bolivia resumed some of the mechanisms of the free market, a group of new industrialists was created by a lavish set of government inducements, including tariff and tax concessions, and a multiple exchange rate that facilitated importation of capital goods. Seldom in the history of Spanish America was the 'money of power' principle used more effectively in winning over emergent capitalists to the government.

By 1964, when the military ousted Paz Estenssoro just before he was to begin a third term to which he had been elected through an obviously rigged balloting process, the Bolivian revolution had lent enormous impetus to a capitalist sector within the dominant culture, while encouraging the sub-culture to persist in its non-capitalist milieu. An ingenious apparatus had been assembled to assure an untroubled relationship between the two cultures. Furthermore, in case overt repression might at some time prove necessary, the MNR, unknowingly sealing its own doom, had reinstated the regular armed forces in their old position of power, after initially eliminating them. Through these and other features of their revolution, Bolivians had hit upon the means for preserving the traditional society.

After seizing political control the military made some small alterations in the apparatus established by the MNR. But in essence it remained intact. Apparently the officers, who have been vying with each other for power since 1964, wish the apparatus to produce essentially the same social results as those intended by the civilians who designed it.

There follows next the story of two Spanish American republics which, unlike Mexico and Bolivia, did not allow tensions within the established order to build up to the point of creating a revolutionary situation – at least not as of the 1960s. Through major modifications – largely fortuitous in the case of Venezuela but often consciously contrived in Uruguay – the leaders of these republics managed to preserve many of the distinctive features of the traditional society.

6 Preserving the Traditional Society through Major Innovations i: The Case of Venezuela

To a degree unmatched in other Spanish American republics, the Venezuelan upper classes have throughout the years been in a state of flux. From the very moment independence was gained from Spain in 1821, Venezuela has been dominated by successive groups of *nouveaux riches* and by men recently risen to political power. The continual evolution in the ranks of the leadership has often been either produced or accompanied by political instability, by *coups* (termed *golpes de estado* in the Spanish-speaking world) and acts of violence. But the steady rise of new groups to power has contributed consistently to social stability by minimizing the likelihood of the long-term alienation of ambitious men. Individual Venezuelan leaders have indeed frustrated the ambitions of many citizens, but it has been enough to remove the particular leader and his immediate collaborators to rectify this situation. There is nothing inherent in the Venezuelan socio-economic and political system that obstructs social mobility and thwarts the realization of lofty ambitions by men born into positions barely on the periphery of political influence, social acceptance and material comfort.

The circumstances that brought about this process of continuous social evolution – a process clearly not conducive to social revolution – owe little to the schemes and programmes of reformers. Rather they were shaped, as the early history of Venezuela shows, by instinctive responses to a historical reality that seemed beyond the power of men to control.

Long before the wars of independence, most of Venezuela's pure-blooded Indians had disappeared as the consequence of Spanish exploitation, disease and miscegenation which produced a mestizo population. Especially in the seventeenth century many African slaves had been imported to work on cacao plantations, and soon they became a new ingredient in a process of racial mixture that witnessed the crossing of African, Spanish and mestizo blood. A good number of the mixed blood *castas* (generally referred to as *pardos* in Venezuela) managed to escape the forced labour status that landowners sought to impose upon them by fleeing to the inaccessible recesses of the interior plains or *llanos*. Surviving in part by cattle-raising, they became a semi-nomadic group of plainsmen or *llaneros*, similar in some ways to the famed *gauchos* of the Argentinian pampa. The predominantly dark-skinned *llaneros*, who provided the all-important manpower for the patriotic forces in the later stages of the wars of independence, staked out lavish rewards for themselves in the new republic. Many of them rubbed shoulders socially and shared political power with the *criollo* aristocracy of Caracas, whose ranks had been decimated by the high casualty rates in the protracted struggle for independence.

Simón Bolívar, the great Venezuelan Liberator, at one time declared: 'The blood of our people is different; we will mix it so as to unite it.' As early as the 1830s an observer in Caracas could attest that Venezuelans were acting in the manner foreseen and favoured by Bolívar. Probably in no other country did the independence movement provide such a stimulus to the mixture of classes and races.

25 Engraving commemorating Simón Bolívar (1783–1830), chief architect of the independence movement in Spain's American empire. One of the first successful indigenous revolutionary leaders of a colonial independence movement (though he ultimately grew apprehensive over the consequences of his accomplishments), Bolívar is hailed by his admirers as the liberator of Venezuela, Colombia, Ecuador, Peru and Bolivia.

Augusto Mijares, one of his country's finest historians, voiced the conviction of many Venezuelan intellectuals when he asserted in 1963 that the land of Bolívar is unique in the entire New World in its natural inclination towards racial equality. Certainly events of the second half of the nineteenth century, building upon those of an earlier period, seem to confirm this judgment. To begin with, there was the sanguinary Federal War (1858–63). Those who supported the federal cause against a centralist power group from Caracas were largely the *pardos* of the interior. In addition, the ranks of the federalists were swelled by many pure-blooded Africans, some of them recently liberated slaves – Venezuela freed its last 12,500 or so slaves in 1854. When the federalist cause triumphed, many of its dark-skinned adherents gained not only extensive landholdings, but high political office as well. The former slave José Félix Mora, for example, became president of the department of Carabobo. Far more so than in other Spanish American countries, class and status in Venezuela after the Federal War came to be determined by economic factors, not by skin colour and family background.

Not long after the war Antonio Guzmán Blanco came to power, ushering in an eighteen-year period (1870–88) of order, progress and prosperity. Although vain and corrupt, Guzmán Blanco – one of the several titles he assumed was 'Illustrious American' – initiated many far-sighted policies that contributed to national development; and he appeared to be free of racial and social prejudices. In fact, this Venezuelan strongman seemed to prefer *pardos* and men of humble origins for important political posts. Opportunities for the country's lowly born were expanded by the funds that Guzmán Blanco lavished on education. Within the first three years of his régime, the government established one hundred new schools in order to provide free and compulsory primary education in accordance with a recently enacted statute.

Although a process of racial and social amalgamation continued to change the composition of the ruling classes during the age of Guzmán Blanco, Venezuela preserved some of the basic characteristics of a two-culture society. The rapidly expanding system of public education was at least partially responsible for this.

In the state-supported primary schools, attended mainly by children of the humble classes because the well-to-do still considered the use of private institutions a status symbol, especial emphasis was placed upon imparting to students a reverential respect for the national heroes of the independence period. By means of this newly fostered nationalism, Venezuelan youth was exhorted to accept sacrifices in the interest of national development, and thus assure the fatherland a future that would match the glories of its past. Students, moreover, were called upon to emulate national heroes who, in the mythology concocted to glorify them, appeared as totally selfless and thoroughly unconcerned with economic reward. Properly indoctrinated students in the emerging Venezuela would, it was hoped, show as much indifference to individual gain and profit as previous generations of lower-class youths inculcated by the Catholic Church with a sense of resignation and the values of other-worldliness. The assault led by Guzmán Blanco against Church privileges in one of the most blatantly anti-clerical programmes in the entire continent was not intended to transform the sort of social structure that the Church had defended through the years. Instead, the assault manifested the president's shrewd perception of the need in an increasingly secular age to devise means independent of traditional religion to maintain the traditional society.

Guzmán Blanco's policies directed against the Catholic Church also stemmed from his desire to encourage the spread of Protestantism among the country's well-to-do elements. As every student of intellectual history knows, debate has long raged over whether a 'Protestant ethic' encourages the rise of industrial capitalism while traditional Catholicism impedes the process. Whatever the merits of the case may be, Spanish American *pensadores* have widely assumed that Protestantism does indeed encourage

26 Antonio Guzmán Blanco (1828–99), the 'Illustrious American'; this vainglorious but complex and controversial leader nourished Venezuelan nationalism, fostered administrative reform and educational expansion, and stimulated economic development.

individualistic, capitalist values. Catholic traditionalists have lamented Protestantism's alleged role, while liberal anti-clericals have applauded it. Guzmán Blanco falls in the latter category. He felt that by facilitating the spread of Protestantism among the upper ranks of Venezuelan society – though significantly not among the masses – he was contributing to his country's material development.

Protestantism, as it turned out, had little impact upon the moneyed classes in Venezuela. But, whereas Protestantism failed to accomplish what Guzmán Blanco expected of it, positivism exceeded his hopes. While the children of the humble in the public primary schools were urged to model their lives upon the example of allegedly self-sacrificing and economically unambitious heroes, the sons of the privileged who went on to the higher levels of education, especially those who attended the Central University of Caracas, embraced the positivist religion of material progress.

Introduced into Venezuela by men such as Rafael Villavicencio and Adolfo Ernst (a German immigrant who arrived in 1861), positivism enjoyed almost the status of an official ideology during the rule of the 'Illustrious American'. Venezuelan positivists stressed that national development depended upon individual, material gain by the country's emerging bourgeois elements. Out of Venezuela's higher institutions of learning, therefore, emerged an unabashedly materialistic generation that equated the lust for private profit with civic virtue and with patriotic concern for the nation's future. Even today, Venezuelans of the upper and middle classes remain among the most overt and self-acknowledged bourgeois materialists in all Spanish America. This fact, in itself a striking departure from the traditional patterns of social structure in the Hispanic world, makes it difficult to distinguish between the bourgeois and the upper-class elements within the dominant culture of Venezuela. On the contrary, its most striking feature is the degree of fusion that obtains among its members, a fusion resulting not from the 'aristocratizing' of the values of the bourgeoisie but rather from the *embourgeoisement* of the values of the aristocracy.

Through a revolution in 1899, following an era of political chaos that began with the fall of Guzmán Blanco, Cipriano Castro initiated what Venezuelan historians refer to as the *sesenta*: a sixty-year period dominated by men from the mountainous, far-western region of Táchira. One of the main features of the *sesenta* was the weakening of the power and prestige of the established élite in Caracas, which in its own turn had ousted an earlier clique which had come to power in the aftermath of the Federal War. Previously a racial melting pot, Caracas now became a geographic melting pot as well, as men who had previously confined their attention to the regional affairs of western Venezuela forced their way into a position of national pre-eminence.

In 1908 the men of Táchira fell out among themselves and Juan Vicente Gómez, soon to be known as 'El Rehabilitador', ousted Castro, whose title had been 'El Restaurador'. Many historians refer to Gómez as an infamous dictator; and they have good grounds for doing so. To quell political opposition, sometimes real, sometimes the product of a paranoid imagination, Gómez jailed Venezuelans in unprecedented numbers. Some prisoners died under torture, many more from being forced to labour under inhuman conditions on the construction of a modern road system in which Gómez took great pride. Corrupt and lecherous, the dictator accumulated a private fortune estimated at some $200 million and fathered a bevy of illegitimate children thought to number between 150 and 200.

Gómez has also been called a nation-builder; and this designation is also not altogether unjustified. Even the generally unadmiring Venezuelan historian Ramón Díaz Sánchez credits the dictator with having ended feudalism by eliminating the local and regional *caudillos* (chieftains or bosses) who had previously kept many areas of the country in a state of isolated, personal rule. Moreover, the income of the national treasury for the period between 1920 and 1930 was 114 per cent higher than for the decade 1910–20. However, this increase was due far more to the discovery of petroleum than to Gómez's qualities as a nation-builder. By 1928 Venezuela had become the world's leading petroleum exporter. Nearly half of the country's oil at this time was produced by the Creole Petroleum Corporation, a subsidiary of Standard Oil of New Jersey.

Among Venezuelans the debate over whether Gómez is more aptly described as an infamous dictator or a nation-builder reflects an ideological cleavage already apparent by the turn of the century. Positivism was then the main intellectual force in the country; but two distinct schools had formed, one optimistic, the other pessimistic. The optimists believed that the people, including the lower classes, could be uplifted and a process of indefinite progress could be inaugurated by means of a transformation of the country's cultural environment and institutions, to be initiated through industrialization. The pessimists, on the other hand, maintained that the bad customs of the masses were the result of racial and geographic factors and were largely irremediable. Possibilities for development were therefore limited, and to prevent Venezuelans from destroying themselves in a vortex of unrestrained passions benevolent dictatorship was a permanent necessity. The optimists judged Gómez harshly, as he certainly showed no interest in transforming the masses. The pessimistic positivists, however, for whom Laureano Vallenilla Lanz was a leading spokesman, held that Gómez provided the country with the most suitable type of rule.

Under Gómez, the masses were on the whole ignored. But there were important exceptions to this pattern. For example, Gómez called off his

27 Material progress and ruthless repression of dissent characterized the régime of President Juan Vicente Gómez (1857–1935), 'El Rehabilitador' to his sycophantic partisans, the reprehensible 'Tyrant of the Andes' to his foes.

country's long-standing anti-clerical movement, heaped favours upon the Catholic Church, and encouraged it to establish a presence among the masses so as to perform various services and spread the gospel of resignation and social solidarity. Moreover, in dealing with the lower classes, the dictator was to some degree benevolent, for he introduced at least a few measures of state paternalism. Gómez did not, however, concern himself with educating the masses; probably he believed they were ineducable. Between 1889 and 1932 only twenty-three public schools were constructed, in contrast to the one hundred opened during the first three years of Guzmán Blanco's rule.

Apparently the masses did not object to the abandonment of government attempts to educate them, so long as the state maintained certain paternalistic programmes designed to supply their basic material needs. In any event Gómez, throughout his twenty-seven year dictatorship, enjoyed considerable popularity at the grass roots. The masses undoubtedly felt that during this time they were treated as well as any other element of society. Well they might, for it was the more prominent Venezuelans, the intellectuals and the men of established families and wealth, rather than the humble, who were the victims of the numerous atrocities and rank injustices perpetrated by the dictatorship. Perhaps the spectacle of the mighty being humiliated brought occasional gratification to the under-privileged and strengthened their devotion to the established order. Certainly, at a much earlier time throughout a large part of the Hispanic world, the Inquisition had in this very manner augmented the Crown's legitimacy among the lower classes.

Acting in line with well established precedents, Gómez saw to it that paternalistic gestures towards the masses imposed no burdens upon the men of means who retained his favour. The government at the time commanded a steadily mounting income that did not depend upon internal capital formation. 'El Rehabilitador', it is true, demanded very little by way

28 Venezuela's prosperity is founded on oil, first exploited on a large scale in the 1920s – in the sixteenth century it had been used to treat the Emperor Charles V's gout: seen here, storage-tanks and living-quarters of the Creole Petroleum Corporation, a subsidiary of Standard Oil of New Jersey.

of tax payments in his concessions to foreign oil companies. Still, he did collect from the foreign firms nearly all that was needed to finance his relatively unambitious social programmes.

If Gómez left those of his countrymen whom he happened at a given moment to favour largely free from burdens and in fact made them the recipients of generous privileges, even these favoured few remained apprehensive because of the dictator's notoriously arbitrary ways. Moreover, Gómez declined to play the part of a moderator between different ideological and political groups. He sought instead to stifle any form of intellectual expression save that which was sycophantic in content; and he prevented the formation of virtually any kind of political association. Because he relied upon brutal authoritarianism, Gómez undermined his legitimacy among large numbers of Venezuelans of the upper and middle classes. If those who were alienated by his methods of rule had been given a chance to vent their pent-up fury, it would not have been surprising if violence and a bloodbath of frightening proportions had resulted.

That this outcome was avoided can be attributed in large measure to the political sagacity of Eleazar López Contreras, also from Táchira and for many years one of Gómez's favourite henchmen. Succeeding to the presidency upon the dictator's death in 1935, López ruled until 1941. Wisely, he permitted those of his countrymen who had long nourished resentment, often while in jail or in exile, to form a number of political and labour organizations. Government came to rest once more upon the exercise of a moderating power rather than upon authoritarianism. Not that the partisans of the deceased dictator were eliminated from positions of power and influence; but they now constituted merely one element in a governing class that encompassed numerous groups of previously repressed intellectuals, professional men and businessmen. Under these circumstances different groups within the dominant culture began to reconcile their differences and to find a working consensus.

The situation altered slightly in the 1940s with the appearance of a new and to some extent a mass party. Acción Democrática (AD), founded in 1941 principally through the efforts of Rómulo Betancourt and Raúl Leoni, both of whom had spent the latter part of the Gómez régime in exile, gained a share of power in the military-civilian junta that governed the country between 1945 and 1948. Taking advantage of its first experience of power, the AD initiated a harsh programme of reprisals against its political foes. When this was followed up by an unrealistic and basically unpopular attempt to liquidate the traditional armed forces, the result was the overthrow in 1948 of the well known novelist Rómulo Gallegos, the AD standard-bearer who had been installed in the presidency earlier in the year.

29 President Marcos Pérez Jiménez (fifth from left), a heavy-handed, lacklustre and (by the standards of the 1950s in Spanish America) rather conventional military dictator, whose social projects in Caracas won him widespread support among the poorer classes whom actually he disdained.

After a period of rule by a military junta, Major Marcos Pérez Jiménez seized power in 1952 and governed dictatorially until 1958. Somewhat in the mould of Gómez, Pérez Jiménez, the last in the dynasty of men from the west who had wielded power since 1899, brutally suppressed political foes. Also like Gómez, he spent only a niggardly percentage of national income on education. But, to a far greater degree than Gómez, Pérez Jiménez inaugurated an extensive programme of social services and fringe benefits for urban workers. Financing presented no difficulty, for ever since the mid-1940s a fifty-fifty agreement had been in operation with foreign oil companies. According to its terms, company profits could not exceed government revenues from the petroleum industry. Between 1943 and 1956, according to Edwin Lieuwen, government income from the oil industry totalled $5300 million. However painless it was for him to assume the role of the generous patron of the masses, about whose inferiority he apparently had few doubts, Pérez Jiménez gained a considerable following among the urban poor, one which he would continue to hold long after his fall from power.

The mid- to late 1950s proved a bad period for military dictators in Spanish America; and Pérez Jiménez was among the several ousted from power at that time. Those who coalesced in the movement to overthrow him included leaders of the Catholic Church, intellectuals, members of political associations that had been outlawed, university students and many professional people. Like Gómez before him, Pérez Jiménez had alienated significant elements within the ruling classes; unlike his predecessor, the rotund and drab military officer was destroyed by those he had dealt with in cavalier fashion.

Once again prominent Venezuelans came together at the end of a dictatorship and found a working consensus. The electorate, although split into several fairly large parties, none of which could capture an absolute majority, maintained a political dialogue. Thus Acción Democrática, triumphing in the first two presidential elections following the fall of Pérez Jiménez, benefited from the occasional co-operation of many of its opponents, including that of the Christian Democratic Party, known in Venezuela as COPEI. The process of political conciliation was facilitated by the country's continuing prosperity based, from the 1950s, not only on petroleum but on huge iron deposits and other natural resources. Singularly favoured by nature, Venezuela, with a population of around 9 million,

30 The Simón Bolívar centre in Caracas commemorates Venezuela's national founder, its modernity at the same time boosting the prestige of the régime.

could by the 1960s boast a per capita income of approximately $800, an unprecedented figure among Spanish American republics – and one which, precisely because it is unprecedented, suggests that Venezuela's methods for assuring social solidarity could hardly be emulated by her sister republics.

Having acquired maturity and moderation during their years of persecution at the hands of Pérez Jiménez, the leaders of AD governed with a relatively high degree of statesmanship, first with Betancourt as president between 1959 and 1964, then with Leoni for a five-year term. By acting as brokers between various ideological and political groups, by exercising a moderating power, Betancourt and Leoni acquired legitimacy for the government once again, if not always popularity for AD, among the upper ranks of society. The AD administrations spent well over 15 per cent of national income on education, which helped win it the support of many of those on the lower fringes of the dominant culture who saw in education an avenue of upward social mobility. One important segment of the middle sector, moreover, the oilfield workers, continued to show a high regard for the established order as their fringe benefits and real wages increased even above the previously high levels. A true labour élite, and among the best paid workers in the world, Venezuela's oilfield labourers were almost without a counterpart in Spanish America. They perform menial tasks and yet enjoy respectability, middle-class status and a real sense of identification with the values of a basically bourgeois dominant culture.

31 Oil drill on Lake Maracaibo. By 1966 Venezuela had become the world's largest producer of oil, which in that year accounted for over 90 per cent of her exports.

Among the lower classes the government enhanced its legitimacy by dramatically augmenting the social services, some of which were administered by a trade-union organization partially under government control. The two successive AD administrations also undertook an imposing agrarian reform, thus benefiting the *campesinos* who were the mainstay of the party's support. The country's moneyed classes could scarcely object to these reforms which cost them little if anything in the form of direct taxes. Steadily pushing beyond 50 per cent its share of the profits generated by foreign oil concerns (plans call for their complete nationalization by the mid-1980s), the government has not had to call upon national capitalists to make sacrifices in financing its social programmes. Thus the members of the dominant culture, without having to pay the premiums on the social stability insurance of government paternalism, can present the appearance to those below them of being generously disposed and altogether willing to be depended upon.

A revolutionary situation could not be even dimly perceived in Venezuela in the late 1950s and the 1960s. Despite threats from guerrilla terrorists, among whom agents from Castro's Cuba were active, to assassinate all those who voted in the 1964 presidential election, 94 per cent of the electorate turned out to cast their ballots and to give an overwhelming endorsement to the parties committed to working within the established system. The election of COPEI standard-bearer Rafael Caldera in 1969, moreover, signified the desire of Venezuelans to avoid drastic departure from the social, economic and political patterns established after the fall of Pérez Jiménez.

Through a series of innovations, the seeds for which were planted fortuitously during the nineteenth century and even earlier, and as a result of a financial capacity provided by unique natural endowments, Venezuela made some major departures from the traditional society, as it functioned elsewhere in Spanish America, without the need for a revolution. Nevertheless, in spite of its innovations, it had not departed from a social structure characterized to some extent by the harmonious functioning of two distinct cultures, one dominant, the other subordinate.

32, 33 Two works by the eminent Uruguayan painter Pedro Figari (1861–1938) recall the traditional two-culture society of the artist's childhood: above, *Going for a Walk*, and, below, *A Negro Dance*.

7 Preserving the Traditional Society Through Major Innovations ii: The Case of Uruguay

In Uruguay, the means used to preserve certain features of traditional society were different from those that operated in Venezuela. Here there were a number of major innovations that were often quite carefully planned; but the result was that Uruguay, at least up to the post Second World War era, seemed to have been as successful as Venezuela in avoiding a revolutionary situation.

In rural Uruguay, as the twentieth century began, social conditions had remained relatively unchanged from colonial times. Two worlds existed side by side, the one the world of the *estancieros* or large estate owners, the other that of the serfs. The landowners avoided modernizing production techniques, in part because they could afford to be indifferent to their estates as a result of their mounting involvement in urban enterprises. In addition they feared that modernization would entail transforming serfs into wage-earners. Through the years they had come to rely on a virtually unpaid labour force to compensate for inefficiency in management and production techniques.

During the first half of the twentieth century, rural Uruguay clung to its traditional ways. It presented a sharp contrast to the capital city of Montevideo, where as early as 1900 over 30 per cent of the population lived and where by the 1960s nearly 50 per cent of the 2·8 million Uruguayans resided. Here important changes were under way.

The process of change in Montevideo gathered unprecedented momentum during the first presidential term of José Batlle y Ordóñez (1903–07). Founder of the newspaper *El Día*, which reflected an agnostic position often attacked by Catholics as atheistic, Batlle described Uruguayan society as divided between those who had more than they deserved and those who deserved more than they had. Accordingly he championed sweeping political and social reforms aimed at bringing about the redistribution of income.

In his first term Batlle's main triumphs lay in the field of political reform. Free elections, based on the secret ballot and a broad expansion of the suffrage, were introduced, together with a system of proportional representation that quickly encouraged an amazing proliferation of political splinter

85

groups. From this time onwards Uruguayans began to regard themselves as the inventors of true democracy in the New World, a status which they assumed gave them the right to upbraid sister republics that had not been able to place their political houses in order. Not without reason has Uruguay frequently been compared to Switzerland.

During his second term (1911–15) Batlle presided over the implementation of far-reaching social and economic reforms, including workmen's compensation and unemployment insurance, as well as generous pension and retirement plans. An ever-expanding bureaucracy administered the comprehensive welfare system and in the process gained control over labour unions which proved willing to surrender to the state all semblance of independent power in exchange for guaranteed security for their rank and file members.

The second Batlle administration also began to establish control over the private capitalist sector and undertook various business activities, maintaining that in this way it would acquire the experience necessary to determine what constituted a just profit. With this experience to guide it the government would be in a position, according to Batlle's supporters, to regulate private firms, especially foreign enterprises, through a taxation policy designed to milk off excess profits.

In the years following the second Batlle administration, successive Uruguayan governments proceeded to expand the political and socio-economic policies introduced by the reforming president. Before long, their welfare state was hailed as a model that other Spanish American countries might well emulate if they desired to avoid social revolution. The essence of the new Uruguay was generally recognized as government paternalism or *bondad* (goodness), the latter a favourite word of Martín C. Martínez, an important minister during the first Batlle régime and, despite his earlier infatuation with Spencerian positivism, one of the architects of state intervention.

As a result of the innovations introduced by Batlle, the vast majority of Uruguayans living in Montevideo tended to coalesce into a single culture. There were, of course, many gradations within it; but even the élite, and still more decidedly the middle sectors, accepted some degree of dependence upon the government and the various programmes of concessions and fringe benefits that assured their economic security. At the same time they turned away, at least to some degree, from competitive individualism. In eighteenth-century Spain and in nineteenth-century Spanish America many would-be reformers had complained that Church-administered charity encouraged the lower classes to remain indifferent to economic productivity and the profit motive. A similar attitude prevailed among all classes in twentieth-century Montevideo on a scale that was unique. Many observers of

Uruguay's capital city in the period between the two world wars complained that government benevolence encouraged all elements of society, not only the poor, to eschew an individualistic, competitive, capitalist ideology.

It would be a flagrant exaggeration to assert that all concern with self-reliance and personal profit was snuffed out among the more affluent members of Montevideo society. What is more – and this perhaps is what above all else rendered the situation unprecedented within the Spanish American context – even those near the bottom of the social ladder enjoyed an increase in real wages and benefited from protective measures that enabled them to accumulate capital and expand their purchasing power. To a limited degree, therefore, the characteristic Spanish American dichotomy between a sub-culture and a dominant culture was eliminated as the lower classes acquired some of the privileges and powers and assumed some of the attitudes of the more privileged class. Certainly, the cultural patterns began to lose some of their more readily discernible identifying traits. The way of life of both the upper and the lower classes was changing, and in the process they were approximating more closely to each other. As a result Uruguay, or more accurately its capital city, seemed to be moving away from the traditional social structure.

The fact was that the uncontrolled pursuit of material gain and individualistic capitalism would have threatened the successful operation of Uruguay's new welfare state. To curb material ambition among all classes of Montevideo society, the government came to rely upon a complex series of non-material rewards and gratifications. For example, pride in the country's democratic institutions, a pride carefully nourished by government propaganda and education, formed the basis of a robust nationalism among Uruguayans and compensated citizens for the sacrifice of some of the benefits ordinarily associated with the competitive pursuit of money. Furthermore, with the division of the country's two major parties into literally scores of splinter groups, each citizen was guaranteed a voice and participation within a subsidiary association that he found natural and congenial and that often reflected not only his ideological values but also defended the special interests of his functional group. Participating within the appropriate corporate bodies, citizens gained the inward satisfaction, the fulfilment, dignity and importance that stem from active political life.

At the same time the Uruguayan political system had built-in screening mechanisms. These, according to its defenders, ensured that only the best men from each of the tiny political splinter groups, chosen by their immediate peers who were in the best position to judge their abilities, would emerge as candidates for national office. To this extent the Uruguayan democratic system was conducive to rule by a select few.

34 Until the 1960s, Uruguay was one of the most stable Spanish American states: this wood engraving by Carlos González shows voters going to the poll in the 1938 presidential election, in which the moderate dictatorship of Gabriel Terra was replaced by Alfredo Baldomir's reckless extension of the government paternalism initiated by Batlle y Ordóñez.

Uruguayans as different as the extremely anti–clerical Martín Martínez, a former positivist, and Mariano Soler, who became the first Archbishop of Montevideo in 1882, had recommended a corporative structure as the best basis for the organization of society. In a way that neither could have foreseen, or would have fully approved, Uruguayans had hit upon a semi-corporative structure that minimized the alleged levelling tendencies of direct democracy.

A further factor that gave Uruguayans a sense of satisfaction was their splendid educational system. With the accomplishments of the late nineteenth-century educational reformer Pedro José Varela as the starting-point, the government of the new Uruguay afforded its citizens, at least those residing in Montevideo, the most accessible and extensive public-school system in the whole of Spanish America. The disciples of Krause and of Rodó could not have failed to approve the emphasis that the public educational system in Uruguay attached to spiritual and aesthetic matters. Moreover, concerts and other cultural and aesthetic events were made readily available to the inhabitants of Montevideo, and they could find additional pleasure in frequenting the nearby beaches, world renowned for their beauty (and indeed were encouraged to do so by the fact that most offices closed shortly after noon during the summer months). A further source of gratification was the succession of fine football teams that were usually close to and sometimes at the very top of the world league.

Life in Uruguay had become to some degree like the life desired by the nobility of sixteenth-century Spain, from the highest grandee down to the *hidalgos*. At least in Montevideo it was possible for a large majority to live in style and dignity, indulging occasionally in conspicuous consumption, without demeaning themselves by becoming directly involved in business or other primary economic activity. The huge and ever expanding government bureaucracy furnished the means for many to lead this type of existence. It goes without saying that the financial demands of the new Uruguay were considerable. But until Batlle died in 1929 – fully satisfied with the success of the system he had helped to devise – these demands could be met through taxes levied upon the foreign controlled sector of the economy, particularly the meat-processing plants. Thus Uruguayans, barring a drastic collapse in world prices for meat and for their other principal exports of wool and hides, seemed to have escaped direct taxation. Within the Hispanic world, exemption from direct taxation was the time-honoured badge of aristocratic status.

In his best known work Rodó praised Ariel as the creature who recognized the primacy of spiritual over material gratification, while Caliban, the dehumanized being concerned mainly with pleasures of the flesh, was depicted as a model to be rejected. In a way the new Uruguay, or more accurately its capital city, fused and synthesized the Ariels and the Calibans. People were encouraged and given the opportunity to pursue the spiritual, cultural, aesthetic pleasures symbolized by Ariel. At the same time they were afforded some taste of the bourgeois, materialistic gratifications that obsessed Caliban. But they were not called upon to develop the character traits or to embrace the values generally assumed to be essential for generating the capital necessary to support the creature-comforts of bourgeois existence.

This was the fatal weakness of the new Uruguay. As foreign enterprises, especially in meat-processing, were harried out of the country in the 1940s and 1950s because of soaring taxes and increasing restrictions, Uruguay had to rely increasingly on deficit financing to meet the costs of its social service. Major crises developed in the 1950s as per capita gross national product failed to rise and the average productivity of labour declined. Protected behind towering tariff walls that guaranteed it a monopoly over the local market, Montevideo's industry remained highly inefficient. Moreover, it was burdened by high labour costs and by payroll taxes of well over 30 per cent, a consequence of the government's desperate attempt to gather revenue with which to support the social services. Approximately half the active labour force was employed in service industries, mainly in the government bureaucracy, and thus contributed little to direct economic production. As workers continued to retire at the age of fifty, often on full pay with adjusted cost of living increases, the government found itself ever more hard pressed to meet its commitments. To compound difficulties, the backward, inefficient rural economy constituted a serious impediment to national development. In the middle of the 1960s there were fewer head of cattle in the country than at the turn of the century. ·

With a deteriorating economy, many of Montevideo's workers found the security they had once enjoyed seriously jeopardized. In fact, the circumstances in which they found themselves threatened to reduce them to the level of a sub-culture in which they would be solely dependent upon the largesse of government. Furthermore, the moneyed classes were unwilling to undertake the obligation of supporting the masses. Apparently only authoritarian measures could induce them to accept the tax burdens that would enable the state to provide at least a minimal subsistence for the working population. This is perhaps understandable, since over the course of nearly half a century they had come to regard government as an instrument that gave to them without asking of them.

By the end of the 1950s the situation in Uruguay was parlous and in the following decade organized violence, countered by government repression, became almost a way of life, as urban guerrillas calling themselves the *tupamaros* carried out a campaign of terrorism in Montevideo. Sources of national pride dried up, for Uruguayans could no longer point to the success of their social institutions in maintaining order and stability. Furthermore, the plural executive or *colegiado* (a National Council that exercised the powers customarily assigned to a single president), a distinctive feature of the country's democratic institutions which had once afforded such vast satisfaction to citizens, proved after several experiments to be unworkable and was abandoned in 1965.

By reducing the distinction between the sub- and dominant cultures in the all-important city of Montevideo, Uruguayans in the first half of the twentieth century had contrived in large measure to preserve the values and style of life associated with a traditional society rooted in the Hispanic past. But the system initiated during Batlle's two presidencies no longer functioned adequately as the second half of the century began. As its failure became ever more manifest the country showed signs of approaching a revolutionary situation. Nevertheless, it is still true that the system worked well for nearly fifty years and, by giving enough citizens the sort of existence they desired, postponed the day of reckoning.

Both in Venezuela and in Uruguay, social revolution was avoided because some – but by no means all – of the distinctive features of the two-culture society underwent modifications of considerable importance. In Chile and Peru, however, they remained more or less intact until the 1960s, and comparatively minor alterations of the established order sufficed to avoid a revolutionary situation and to sustain the traditional society.

35 The burnt-out shell of a United States-owned textile factory bears witness to the ferocity of the urban guerrilla warfare waged by the *tupamaros* since the early 1960s in an attempt to precipitate a major social revolution and destroy all vestiges of the capitalist system.

36 Peasants display their support for the Socialist Central Union of Workers. President Salvador Allende, elected in 1970, accelerated the process of land expropriation and redistribution initiated by the Chilean Christian Democrats between 1964 and 1970 and attempted to restructure his country in accordance with his relatively moderate brand of Marxian socialism.

8 Preserving the Traditional Society Through Minor Innovations i: Chile until the 1960s

In 1924 the Chilean military entered directly into the political arena, overthrew the civilian president, and established a junta of high-ranking officers to govern the country. Three years later, after a brief restoration of civilian, constitutional rule, Colonel Carlos Ibáñez del Campo seized the presidency. These acts of military intervention ended a period of constitutional government that had begun in 1830 and had only once, in 1891, been interrupted by a successful political revolution. Behind the rise of militarism lay a social problem that had seriously divided the major political parties.

By the late nineteenth century a demographic shift had begun to offset the tranquillizing effects of the paternalistic *patrón-inquilino* relationship (the latter term in Chilean usage designated rural workers who received the use of land plots in return for their labour) that had historically prevailed in the countryside. Between 1892 and 1920 the Chilean population increased by only half a million, from 3 3 to 3·8 million. But there was a major movement of population from the countryside to the towns. The urban population, only 27 per cent of the total in 1875, had risen to over 43 per cent in 1902.

In the late nineteenth century the owners of large estates in southern and central Chile, hoping to take advantage of the greater world demand for grain by increasing output, had begun to impose more stringent labour obligations on *inquilinos*. As a result many of these serfs or their children abandoned the countryside and flocked into northern and central towns and cities. There they found themselves without even the minimal paternalistic aid that had benefited them in their former rural setting. Even more numerous among the shifting elements of the population were the peons (*gañanes*), formerly seasonal migratory agricultural labourers and often the owners of tiny land parcels, who moved to the cities attracted by the prospects of higher wages. Bewildered and angered by the exploitation to which they were subjected in the new and alien environment, and no longer enjoying even the marginal security that paternalism or the possession of miniscule plots of land had afforded them, the men who had fled the countryside began to demand better treatment from society. Labour unrest, violent

93

strikes and the spread of anarchist and socialist ideas among the urban proletariat of Santiago, Valparaíso and Concepción, as well as among the nitrate workers of the northern desert area with its major cities of Antofagasta and Iquique, had already begun to alarm a few of the more far-sighted political leaders during the first decade of the twentieth century. Alarm grew as the economic dislocation accompanying the First World War led to intensified urban labour violence.

Against this background the *laissez-faire* philosophy of Ramón Barros Luco, president from 1911 to 1915, was no longer acceptable. Barros Luco had declared there were only two kinds of problems, those that solved themselves and those that had no solution. In the immediate aftermath of the war, however, Chileans turned in mounting numbers to the task of problem-solving, anxious to discover the means by which they could maintain most of the traditional features of their political and socio-economic organization.

The Chilean ruling classes, however, were deeply divided in their approach to their country's problems. As J. O. Morris has pointed out, on one side was the Conservative Party, closely affiliated with the Roman Catholic Church, influential members of which urged the creation of company unions through which the paternalism once practised by land-owners in dealing with *inquilinos* could be adapted to an urban, incipiently industrialized setting. Social justice was to be based upon the teachings of the Church which, in alliance with the propertied classes, would establish guide-lines for implementing new charitable programmes. On the other side, the Liberal Party and its political allies advocated the formation of a government controlled, nation-wide labour union through which a centralized bureaucracy, absolutely free from any connection with the Church, would extend various economic concessions to the working classes.

In the presidential election of 1920 the Liberal candidate, Arturo Alessandri Palma, triumphed by a narrow margin, but the Conservatives maintained a sizable congressional bloc. The new president, unable to obtain parliamentary agreement as to the type of social and labour legislation that should be enacted, and further handicapped because many deputies and senators saw no need to modify even slightly the classical liberal approach, made little headway in the first four years of his term in fulfilling his campaign promises.

As social discontent mounted in the face of government inactivity, the military resorted to direct political action and overthrew Alessandri in 1924, well before the end of his five-year term. One of the most important consequences of intervention by the armed forces was the enactment of social and labour legislation that embodied some elements of both the

Conservative and Liberal programmes. Thereupon the soldiers returned to the barracks. But the subsequent inability of the civilian administrators to implement the new legislation provided Carlos Ibáñez, the minister of war, with justification for seizing power in 1927.

Never a theorist, Ibáñez was a consummate master of the art of political manœuvre and of blending the ideas of others. While he did not shy away from the occasional use of force, he possessed the redeeming feature of moderation. In addition, he introduced a high tone of nationalism into Chilean politics. Instead of resorting to demagogic promises, he called upon the masses for sacrifice and work.

Under Ibáñez a national, government controlled labour union was created through which the workers managed to secure slight improvement in their real wages and, more significantly, a wide variety of social services and fringe benefits. To finance his social and public works programmes and some tenuous agrarian reform measures, Ibáñez resorted to foreign loans totalling more than $95 million. The resourceful dictator also obtained revenue through imposts, minimal though they were, on foreign enterprise, which grew rapidly at this time. Between 1925 and 1930, foreign investment in Chile rose from $723 million to $1017 million. In the same period foreign capital, of which the United States accounted for 60 per cent, represented an average of 36 per cent of total annual investment.

Encouraged by the striking success of many of their members during this period in rising to upper-class status, Chile's middle sectors on the whole remained content to serve as the guardians of the aristocracy – even though a Communist Party founded a few years before Ibáñez took over gained some following among intellectuals. From 1925 the middle sectors began to invest in rural property, a process which resulted, within thirty-five years, in a change of ownership of some 60 per cent of the arable land in the fertile central valley. The possession of rural properties gave the new landowners the social prestige necessary to qualify for upper-class status, and their example encouraged other men of the middle sectors to dream of upward social mobility.

The world-wide economic depression of 1929 undermined the successful functioning of Ibáñez's policies. When the depression struck, Chile lost both its markets and ready access to foreign investment and loan capital. Within three years the value of exports declined by over 80 per cent. Because of the economic crisis, the days of the dictatorship were numbered. Faced with a general strike in July 1931, Ibáñez resigned and went into exile. The following months witnessed indescribable political chaos, which came to an end only with military intervention and supervision of a new election towards the end of 1932. The election resulted in an impressive triumph for Arturo Alessandri and heralded Chile's return to constitutional order.

The most notable political development during Alessandri's second term of office was the conclusion of an agreement between Conservatives and Liberals. Long sharing similar beliefs about the necessity of maintaining the established social order, Conservatives and Liberals in the nineteenth and early twentieth centuries had differed mainly over means, over issues between the Church and state, and over whether the ideal society should be confessional or secular. In the early 1930s the Liberals abandoned their customary anti-clericalism and, realizing that the Church could be a valuable ally in the struggle against social change and class conflict, began to co-operate with the political appendage of the Chilean Catholic hierarchy, the Conservative Party – within whose bosom, according to an early enthusiast, a man was closer to God. Soon the two parties were collaborating smoothly in backing the new administration.

Assured in this way of Conservative and Liberal support, Alessandri and his finance minister, Gustavo Ross Santa María, devoted their energies to economic recovery. They developed new industries to reduce imports, and through this import substitution bound old industrialists as well as the new industrial leaders firmly to the government by means of tariff protection and tax incentives. For a time inflationary methods of finance were utilized so that the government might resume the various social services without taxing the well-to-do. By the mid-1930s world prices for copper had begun to rise and this basic industry, largely controlled by United States capital, once more provided revenue with which the government could meet its social obligations.

Gradually re-establishing the power and prestige of the presidency, Alessandri displayed a cunning that bordered on genius as he exercised a moderating power upon the various ideological and political factions into which the Chilean ruling classes were divided. In using his power to safeguard the *status quo* in the difficult years of depression Alessandri, like other Spanish American leaders at the time, was helped by the fact that the advocates of fundamental change were so divided among themselves as virtually to cancel each other out. On the fragmented Left various socialist groups, as well as the Communists, were locked in bitter dispute, at least until the mid- to late 1930s. On the equally divided Right some groups advocated a revitalization of Catholic spiritual values and the establishment of a decentralized corporative state so as to protect the interests of the old-line élite. Others on the Right embraced National Socialism, called for a modernizing revolution largely free from religious influences and directed towards achieving material greatness, and championed a highly centralized corporative state in which power would lie in the hands of a new élite.

The lack of accord among the groups urging sweeping change, whether aimed at returning to the past or entering a bright new future, strengthened the hand of non-ideological, pragmatic conservatives, among whom Alessandri could be counted. Not even the triumph in the 1938 presidential election of the Popular Front, ostensibly an ideologically left-wing alliance, fundamentally altered the situation. The Front's triumph deceived many into anticipating or dreading important changes, but reality was different.

The origins of the Popular Front go back to 1935 when the Chilean Communists, acting in accordance with newly formulated Russian policies, opted, like Communists elsewhere, for a policy of gradualism. Declaring that the time was not yet ripe for a proletarian revolution, they began to seek the co-operation of other groups in pursuing mildly reformist programmes. Two years before this, in 1933, the four most important non-Communist Marxist groups temporarily put aside their acerbic polemics and merged to form the Socialist Party. This uneasy grouping of Marxists continued on the whole to expound the rhetoric of immediate revolution against the capitalist order. Despite many differences between them, Chile's Communist and Socialist Parties had by 1938 agreed upon a political pact. The Popular Front that resulted from this pact also included the Radical Party, made up largely of middle-sector urban interests and including many powerful industrialists. At the time of its founding in the 1860s the Radical Party had propounded the gospel of Adam Smith and Herbert Spencer, but early in the twentieth century it half-heartedly declared in favour of state intervention in economic affairs, which it equated with socialism. This, plus a consistent anti-clericalism, apparently qualified the party for inclusion in a leftist alliance. In addition, the Radical leaders undoubtedly hoped through joining the Front to be in the best position to restrain the Chilean Left and to protect their strong representation in the local and national bureaucracy – considerations that also help to explain their contribution in 1970 to the victory of Salvador Allende.

In retrospect the Popular Front was significant not for radical innovation but for the continuation and extension of the measures introduced by Ibáñez, and maintained during the depression years by Alessandri, for protecting the established order and safeguarding the social system against the challenge of class conflict. During the three years of Front rule, membership in the organized labour movement soared and even real wages for industrial workers increased slightly. Social services were expanded, and impressive housing projects – with units for manual labourers clearly segregated as in the past from those for white-collar workers – and school-building programmes were undertaken. Because demand generated by the Second World War resulted in higher prices for Chilean exports, the government was able to finance its social programmes without resorting to new direct internal taxes.

The patterns of change, designed to prevent fundamental reform, established in Chile in the 1920s developed many weaknesses during the ten years of Radical Party rule which followed the demise of the faction-ridden Popular Front in 1941, and during the lacklustre presidency of Carlos Ibáñez between 1952 and 1958. Still, however impaired their operation became, the mechanisms devised in the 1920s enabled the old order to endure without having to face major crises until the 1960s.

The crises of the 1960s originated in the malaise that gripped Chile's social order, especially during the 1940s and 1950s. This malaise, in turn, was attributable in some ways to the delusions of national pride. According to a sizable number of articulate Chileans, their country is unique among the Spanish American republics in the strength of its democratic, constitutional institutions, created and sustained by a comparatively white population. The allegedly racially inferior countries with huge, unassimilated Indian groups and the tropical, turbulent lands of the Caribbean, with high percentages of Negroes and mulattos, can be expected to suffer revolutionary upheavals. But Chile, according to the nationalists, is different. Therefore, many of its citizens apparently concluded, social problems could be ignored without fear of a major social upheaval.

Another factor affecting the attitude of the Chilean upper classes was the presence of foreign capital. Up to the 1960s, at least, wealthy Chileans believed that foreign capital relieved them of the necessity of making personal sacrifices for the amelioration of social problems. Halfway through the twentieth century, the country's tax structure was still characterized by a heavy dependence on external transactions, including revenue deriving from foreign trade and imposts upon foreign subsidiaries. Between 1946 and 1953, according to the Economic Commission for Latin America, the external sector as a whole produced over one-half, and the United States copper-mining companies around 30 per cent, of the nation's revenue derived from taxation.

Even had revenue from foreign enterprise expanded dramatically, it would not have been sufficient to enable the government to meet its mounting problems. Thus, as the 1960s began, it no longer seemed possible for Chile to continue in its old ways. A warning had come in 1958 when a Marxist dominated alliance failed by only 40,000 votes to elect its standard-bearer, Salvador Allende, president of Chile. The ensuing six years, during which conservative forces continued to dominate the country, witnessed an alarming increase in lower-class discontent. But the main threat to the established order seemed to come from the disaffected members of the middle sectors. This disaffection was a significant factor in the triumph in the 1964 presidential election of the Christian Democrats who promised a 'revolution in liberty'. Chilean sociologist Eduardo Hamuy explains the situation in these words:

The oligarchy always used to absorb the middle classes. . . . They always absorbed every group. . . . Then, after the Second World War, a new middle class began to grow, but now there was no room for them in the upper-class inn. . . . Now they were not absorbed. It was an economic fact. The best businesses were monopolized by the old oligarchy and the first industrialists and there was no great capacity to satisfy the aspirations of the new groups. . . . These people . . . are the leaders of the Christian Democrats.

Complex and often contradictory in its ideology, frequently vague and confusing in its programmes, the Chilean Christian Democratic Party could offer something to almost every conceivable type of supporter. If, for example, someone was disenchanted with the capitalist system, the Party could delight him with the prospects of the *sociedad comunitaria*. To a larger degree than they cared to admit, Christian Democrats were indebted for their ideas in this sphere to the early, revolutionary Falange, the Falange before it was tamed and transformed into a component of a non-revolutionary system by Francisco Franco.

Manifesting the anti-capitalist spirit so widespread in the Hispanic world, the founders of the Spanish Falange had called in the early 1930s for the restructuring of society into joint capital-labour syndicates. Within these syndicates the distinction between capital and labour was little by little to pass away as the two functions came to be combined in the same men. This was to be accomplished through profit-sharing devices resulting in the distribution to members not just of money but of stock in each enterprise. Eventually ownership of each firm would pass to the labourers. In this way private property and capitalism as they had previously existed would disappear. The new system would, hopefully, provide each worker-owner with the bare essentials of what was required to lead a life of modest material comfort; but money accumulating beyond this amount would be taken by the state, in part to supply the needs of worker-owners in enterprises operating at a loss. Essentially this system, which Spanish *Falangistas* called national syndicalism, was what Chilean Christian Democrats had in mind when they referred to the *sociedad comunitaria*.

If, however, a Chilean did not desire the elimination of capitalism, then he could ignore communitarian ideology – not many party leaders took it very seriously – and respond enthusiastically to the Christian Democratic campaign message of 1964 that bourgeois economic expertise and incentives were required if the country was to solve its problems. He could also nod in approval at the frequent pronouncements that creation of capital rather than its redistribution must be the primary concern of national leaders. And he could find additional comfort in the speeches of Christian Democrats

37 Beneath a giant poster of himself, Eduardo Frei (in the 1960s regarded by anti-Marxists within and outside Chile as his country's 'last good hope') appeals for support: his Christian Democratic Party sought new solutions to social problems and attempted to satisfy the demands of a growing middle class.

who urged workers to become more productive and said not a word about their transformation into owners of the enterprises for which they laboured.

If a Chilean was disillusioned by his country's parliamentary system, then he might find some hope for the future in the stress the Christian Democrats placed on what seemed to be the corporative reorganization of society through the creation of semi-autonomous local, regional and functional groups within which decision-making would be left largely to rank and file membership. This feature of their platform the Christian Democrats had borrowed largely from their ideological precursors in Spain who, early in the twentieth century, had formed the Grupo de la

Democracia Cristiana and who advocated the establishment of a parliament based on functional representation. There was, however, considerable ambiguity about what Chilean Christian Democrats expected corporative entities to accomplish when introduced into their country. In any event, if corporativism did not attract them, Chileans could perhaps find something appealing in Christian Democracy's advocacy of a hazily defined type of democratic pluralism that party ideologists had borrowed from the French philosopher Jacques Maritain.

Wracked by internal inconsistencies and always lacking a focus, the Christian Democratic Party began to splinter shortly after coming to power. In spite of this, it made many remarkable accomplishments as it legislated for and then began actually to implement a land reform programme, as it provided for increasing Chilean ownership of the United States dominated copper companies, and as it scored some of the most noteworthy advances in education in the country's history. For these accomplishments the charisma, uncommon ability and unquestioned sincerity of the Christian Democratic president, Eduardo Frei Montalva, were largely responsible. Notwithstanding Frei's hopes of moulding a political organization not based solely on one personality, Chilean Christian Democracy remained less a party than the vehicle of one remarkable statesman who was barred by constitutional provision from serving a second consecutive term.

Despite their accomplishments while in office, the Christian Democrats had not been able to satisfy the expectations they had aroused by their oratory, and they had not been able to effect the basic structural changes in the social and economic order desired by left-wing members of their party. These circumstances contributed to the victory in the 1970 election of Marxist Socialist Salvador Allende, who enjoyed the support of his own political *confrères* and of the Communist and Radical Parties.

After two years in office, Allende was plagued by a variety of economic problems, manifested in part by a decline in agricultural productivity that resulted in serious food shortages and worsening rates of inflation. Agricultural production suffered from the seizure of farm lands carried out by ultra-left groups over which the president could exercise little restraint, and from the failure of many landowners, fearing seizure of their properties, to plant crops. The régime, facing further difficulties because of a decline in copper prices, sought to blame its economic plight on a conspiracy of the leading capitalist nations of the world to block credits, investment funds and trade opportunities in retaliation against the nationalization of foreign enterprises.

At the end of 1972 Allende also faced formidable political problems. The Christian Democrats headed a large and effective congressional opposition

38 Midway in his six-year term, Allende's widespread support among the poor continued to be the mainstay of his government, which faced stiffening opposition from the middle and upper classes.

bloc. Against this background the prediction of Fidel Castro during his 1971 visit to Chile that the defenders of the established order would triumph over the revolutionary forces if Allende remained over scrupulous about observing constitutional procedures seemed to be gaining confirmation. Allende, however, felt constrained to ignore the urgings of extremists within his administration to silence the opposition, fearing that an overt move against constitutional procedures would goad the armed forces into political intervention. All the while, moreover, the deep-seated antagonism between Chile's nationalistic, revolutionary Socialists and the gradualist Communists, an antagonism that had helped doom the Popular Front, created serious divisions within the Allende régime.

Two years after his inauguration Allende appeared still to have a large following among the slum dwellers of Santiago and other lower-class

39 Salvador Allende and Fidel Castro, Spanish America's two Marxist rulers, during the Cuban leader's visit to Chile in November 1971. In January 1973 Allende in his turn visited Castro in Havana.

groups who responded enthusiastically to class-conflict oratory and who were grateful for the free milk which the government had supplied the children of the poor. However, the euphoric mood in which the advocates of revolutionary change had greeted the 1970 electoral results had given way to one that fluctuated between extremely guarded optimism and downright defeatism and despair. Conversely, conservative elements, both within the country and abroad, were beginning to take heart.

Only the most foolhardy of men would venture to predict the outcome of Allende's announced plan to lead Chile, through at least initially democratic methods, into socialism. It is certain, however, that, just as the Christian Democrats before him, he came very quickly to discover the amazing power of the traditional system, despite its many symptoms of malaise, to resist structural change.

40 Map of Central and South America.

9 Preserving the Traditional Society Through Minor Innovations ii: Peru until the 1960s

Crushing defeat at the hands of Chile in the War of the Pacific (1879–83) had cost Peru's ally, Bolivia, its coastal territory. For Peru, it had resulted in the loss of a southernmost region containing some of the continent's richest nitrate resources. Peru, however, emerged from the war with a new national resource, a galaxy of heroes, almost all of whom were renowned principally for the defeats they had sustained. These strange occupants of Peru's pantheon symbolize, for many observers, an abiding national complex of inferiority. Such a complex has been suggested by the Peruvian tendency, especially since the War of the Pacific, to make self-depreciation and an acerbic disparagement of national accomplishments into something of a national pastime. Peruvians, in fact, seem to take a perverse pride in their self-proclaimed inferiority and to have made it a vital ingredient in their myth-fantasy of nationalism.

In so far as the masses venerated them, Peru's unusual set of defeated heroes were able to contribute to the preservation of a tragic sense of life. Their example, after all, can be interpreted as testimony to the inevitability of failure in confronting the problems and challenges of this world and to the grandeur of inward, spiritual growth that can result precisely from that failure. Thus, their example can be so construed as to cast doubt upon the myth of capitalism's success and to discredit the quest for economic gain through competition for material rewards. Moreover, Peru's distinctive myth-fantasy of nationalism that accepts and even extols inferiority may, to the degree that its values have been cultivated among the lower classes, enhance attitudes of fatalistic resignation, contributing thereby to preserving the sub-culture in a state of docile dependence.

As we have already seen, Venezuelans under Guzmán Blanco used a different species of nationalism and a different form of hero-worship to discourage capitalist incentives and attitudes among the masses. Presidents Cárdenas of Mexico and Paz Estenssoro of Bolivia, as well as dictator Ibáñez of Chile, traded upon pride in the nation's destiny to encourage the masses to accept unquestioning dependence on the state at the same time as they were exhorted to contribute to its progress through more efficient labour. It was as if the masses were asked to believe that national independence required and was worth the sacrifice of their own individual independence. And, to a degree perhaps unique in Spanish America, Argentinian leaders at various times in their country's history have sought to compensate the lower classes for their lack of independence with satisfaction in the nation's alleged superiority and its glorious future. This was particularly true during the Perón era, described briefly in the following chapter. However varied its guises, nationalism has been a useful tool in maintaining the dependence of a sub-culture. Perhaps this has been its principal purpose in Spanish America. But adequate investigation of this matter requires the talents of a psychiatrist; and it is safer for a historian seeking to explain the preservation of the traditional society in Peru to take up the narration of events in that country.

Beginning in the mid-1880s, Peruvian administrations undertook the task of recovery from the ravages of war. Aided by the discovery and extraction of silver in the *sierra*, the country's military government achieved some progress towards economic rehabilitation. The process was facilitated by foreign capital made available through an agreement (1889) with British financial interests known as the Grace Contract. For their part, the British capitalists gained long-term control over the Peruvian railways and a temporary monopoly on the guano supply.

In 1895, managing to ally the bitterly antagonistic Democratic and Civilista Parties, and thereupon to overthrow the incumbent military régime, Nicolás de Piérola began a productive four-year term, during which he helped to establish the foundations of a stability destined to endure for some twenty years. Under government stimulus, moreover, Peruvians began to take some faltering steps towards industrial development. A new industrial bourgeoisie, beginning to appear during the Piérola administration, was to demand and to some degree obtain in the years immediately ahead a share, along with the mining and landowning aristocracy, in the control of national policies.

Aroused by signs of progress, certain Peruvian intellectual and political leaders dreamt of transforming their country into an economic giant. Frequently adopting the ideas of reformist positivism, these leaders envisaged the transformation of the masses into individualistic, efficient producers who would also be acquisitive consumers in possession of effective purchasing power. The sociologist Joaquín Capelo spoke for this school when he asserted in the third volume of his *Sociología de Lima* (1900): 'If we wish to be rich and powerful, let us develop within the country frugality, productive aptitudes and individual morality. . . . In Lima every man has the power and the duty to be rich: that is, to be virtuous and enlightened and to enjoy material welfare, thanks to an income earned with honour through hard work and assured by adequate savings.' Manuel Vicente Villarán, a prominent intellectual destined for a distinguished political career, expressed a similar viewpoint in *Las profesiones liberales en el Perú*, a work also published in 1900: 'Only if given education will the lower classes be able to protect themselves and contribute to, because they are sharing in, the increase of national wealth.'

In substance, Capelo and Villarán wished to transform members of the sub-culture – although they did not use the term – of Lima and the urban centres of coastal Peru into effective producers and consumers. Inevitably, other social and economic thinkers turned their attention to the economic potential lying dormant in the highland Indians, who constituted about half the country's total population. The glittering possibilities attendant upon uplifting the Indian sub-culture began to fascinate Peruvians in the period following the War of the Pacific. In the 1920s Luis E. Valcárcel was among the many intellectuals still intrigued by these possibilities. Repeating in 1945 the message he had first begun to propound during the 1920s, Valcárcel wrote in his *Ruta cultural del Perú*:

> Our country will emerge from its feudal, colonial and agricultural state, it will undergo industrialization. In order for this to transpire, there is no need to increase our population by bringing in foreign immigrants . . . ; it is only necessary to utilize the five million Indian workers. . . . Because of an instinctive terror, the populace of coastal Peru has not been willing to acknowledge the tremendous potential of the Indian. But today there are increasing pressures . . . to force Lima to recognize the urgency of achieving national integration by equipping the Indian masses to become a political, economic and cultural factor in Peru.

The reformists' insistence, from before the turn of the century onwards, on transforming the Peruvian sub-culture by forcing its members into the world of values and incentives previously confined to more privileged sectors infuriated other groups of intellectuals. Among them was Manuel González Prada, who as early as the 1880s and 1890s had begun to preach the superiority of the way of life of the lower masses, especially of the Indians, and the need to force the upper classes, by stripping them of their material possessions, to abandon their individualistic, materialistic way of life. His animosity towards the white directing classes of coastal Peru led him to declare that these people combined in the worst possible manner the features of the country's three non-Indian races: white skin, yellow heart, black soul. At first González Prada saw the solution to Peru's problems in socialism, but later he came to believe that anarchism promised the best future for his country. In both his socialist and anarchist stages, this firebrand proclaimed the need for a violent revolution, by means of which the Indian masses of the *sierra* would impose their life style upon the economically developed but allegedly spiritually retarded coastal area.

Taking up some of the ideas of González Prada but adding many new arguments of their own, a group of *indigenista*, socialist admirers of Peru's pre-conquest Inca civilization, began in the 1920s to intensify the demand that all Peru be reformed in line with the values that allegedly still animated the country's Indian masses. The outstanding leader of this school was José Carlos Mariátegui. Struck by the lack of individualistic acquisitiveness among the Indians of highland Peru, by their communal landownership and labour customs, by their ability to find contentment in inward, spiritual rewards rather than in material ones, Mariátegui began to preach a highly unorthodox type of Communism. In his article 'Defensa de Marxismo', published in 1928, Mariátegui propounded a Communism that derived more from the Inca past than from the theories of Marx, Engels and Lenin. A Communism rooted in the Indian past, he avowed, would give 'prodigious impulse to art, religion and philosophy and transport the workers to new heights'. He concluded: 'There is a mysticism in Communism and those who adhere to it come very close to the spirit of the Christianity of the catacombs.'

Apparently what this brilliant and highly original Peruvian *indigenista* desired was the fashioning of a government machinery, patterned after the old Inca bureaucracy, that would capture the individual wealth of Peru's upper class and middle sectors and reduce all citizens to a status of dependence previously reserved only for the Indian masses and, to some extent, for the urban proletariat. By providing for the material needs of citizens, the government envisaged by Mariátegui would liberate them from obsession with individual gain, leaving them free to develop the more exalted resources of human nature. Content with the inward satisfaction thereby derived, Peruvians, in line with the patterns Mariátegui saw in the pre-conquest Inca empire, would accept as natural the fact that they were materially dependent upon and economically subservient to the state apparatus. They would, in short, be willing to live according to the formula: from each according to his abilities, to each according to his needs.

41 José Carlos Mariátegui (1895–1930), Peru's highly original and exceedingly unorthodox Marxist *pensador*, who found in the primitive Communism of Inca civilization models for twentieth-century development. Mariátegui's influence in Andean America has grown since his death and in the 1960s he was hailed as a prophet not only by Marxists of every stripe but also by Catholic champions of social justice.

42 Indians leaving a Roman Catholic church in Cajamarca (the town where Pizarro and his followers captured the Inca ruler Atahuallpa in 1532). The elaborate façade of the church, typical of colonial baroque-rococo architecture, disguises a building of basic simplicity and older styles of design and seems symbolic of the veneer that more than four centuries of dominance by Christian ruling classes have imposed over Indian character and customs.

Violence exploded in the Peruvian Andes during the 1920s, a consequence of incursions made upon Indian communal properties by avaricious private landowners of the *sierra* rather than of the ideas preached by Mariátegui and his associates. Even earlier, the labouring classes of the coast had begun to lash out against a system that, to all intents and purposes, called upon them to solve their problems by their own efforts without relying upon government paternalism, while at the same time withholding from them the means of self-improvement and economic self-reliance. Responding to the call of Marxist and anarchist organizers, the workers showed every sign of espousing a movement intended to reduce the upper ranks of society to poverty. Strikes and labour violence, accompanied by agitation among university students, spread from one end of coastal Peru to the other in 1918 and 1919. A revolutionary situation seemed at hand. If the substance of the traditional social structure were to be preserved, the time had come for the privileged classes to make concessions to the workers.

This was the situation in which Augusto B. Leguía emerged as the master of innovation. Seizing power in 1919 he ruled Peru dictatorially, but with appreciable popular support, for the next eleven years, a period known as the *oncenio*. Indian violence flared sporadically in the far off Andes, but in coastal Peru calm was restored as Leguía introduced a programme of government sponsored and Church backed paternalism that restored to the working classes a sense of security. Workers, moreover, were no longer called upon to reform themselves and to change their ways of life. Instead they were presented with assurances that the state, and its ally the Church, would protect them within their customary mode of existence, by means of a proliferating bureaucracy, a carefully controlled labour organization and Catholic Action programmes. Relieved of the clamorous call to reform, the labouring classes must have experienced a renewed sense of dignity. And, as self-esteem returned, their revolutionary ardour waned. At the same time, Peru's ruling classes quietly abandoned hope of the sort of material progress that might have turned the land into a genuine industrial power. The sacrifice of possibilities for development, based upon the transformation of the masses into capitalists, did not appear too high a price to pay for continued social stability.

Leguía's programme of government paternalism was expensive. Predictably, in order to obtain the funds needed to finance it, the shrewd dictator turned to imposts on the expanding operations of foreign capitalists, especially those from the United States. During the eleven years of his rule United States private investments eclipsed those of Great Britain. By 1925 the investment of the Cerro de Pasco Corporation, dominated by United States capitalists and active in copper-mining and related activities, was conservatively estimated at $50 million. Earlier in the *oncenio* the

International Petroleum Company, a Standard Oil subsidiary, got possession of the La Brea-Pariñas oilfields previously claimed by an English firm.

Besides taxes on foreign trade and investment operations, the Peruvian government depended for its revenue on loans from abroad and deficit financing. Between 1918 and 1929, Peru's foreign debt rose from approximately $10 million to $100 million. Nearly all the foreign loans came from international banking concerns in the United States. Largely because of loans from abroad and deficit financing, the Peruvian budget by 1929 called for an expenditure of approximately $80 million, a figure which exceeded income by a considerable margin and represented nearly a fourfold increase over government outlays in 1920.

If Leguía restored a sense of contentment, and possibly even of dignity, to the labouring masses, and if he won the support of the wealthy by exempting them from contributing personally to his programmes, he also provided new means of economic and social advancement for the middle sectors. In the bureaucracy and in numerous sections of the expanding ancillary services, Peru's middle sectors found plenty of avenues leading towards greater wealth. Himself a man of middle-sector origins, Leguía saw to it that the *nouveaux riches* gained access to bastions of social prestige and political power previously reserved for persons of aristocratic lineage. And, attracted by the magnitude of the fortunes being amassed by men they might otherwise have dismissed as social upstarts, the country's élite formed a number of business and matrimonial alliances with the expanding bourgeoisie.

Not all members of the middle sectors were seduced into support of Leguía's new Peru, dubbed the *patria nueva*. Numerous intellectuals were scandalized by the hypocrisy of a régime that proclaimed its respect for democracy and individual rights, yet systematically practised repression; that preached university reform, yet banished critical professors from the classroom and dealt harshly with dissident students; that advocated decentralization and regional autonomy, yet imposed upon the country the most stiflingly centralized administration it had known since independence; that pledged itself to uplift the descendants of the Incas, yet sent the army into the *sierra* to aid private landowners in plundering Indian communal property. Many of the middle-sector intellectuals who were outraged by this double-dealing found their way into the Alianza Popular Revolucionaria Americana (APRA) founded in 1924 by the former university student leader, Víctor Raúl Haya de la Torre.

There has been no more controversial political movement in the history of Spanish America than APRA. To this day generalizations about it are extremely hazardous and many observers, the present writer included, have come to regret their initial attempts to form a judgment. Nevertheless, it is

43 Víctor Raúl Haya de la Torre (b. 1895), founder of the *Aprista* movement. The initially radical programme of his movement had a crucial influence on Peruvian politics throughout the 1930s; later the opportunistic Haya, destined to remain thwarted in his obsessive quest for political dominance, won new support as he steered APRA into a highly conservative position.

probably reasonably accurate to describe the goal of APRA during its early years as a radical, if necessary violent, revolution led by men of the middle sectors, in the course of which the traditional upper classes would be eliminated, and with them various features of the capitalist system as it had operated until that time. Once in control these middle sectors would resort to a massive programme of education or indoctrination to instil a fervent nationalism in the masses, including the Indians. The *Apristas* hoped that this nationalism would assume the proportions of religious zeal and fanaticism and that it would lead the masses to abandon any materialist or capitalist ambitions they had formed through contact with the pre-revolutionary social elements above them. Instead, according to the *Aprista* plan, they would be satisfied with the moral rewards provided by the new religion of nationalism and would contribute to the common good according to their abilities, while receiving from the state only what was necessary to satisfy their basic needs.

In their plans and hopes for the future, *Apristas* sought to eliminate the national inferiority complex and to replace it with faith in Peru's future greatness. Were the middle sectors, once the revolution had placed its members in control, expected to be satisfied by exercising their power in order to elevate Peru to a position of national grandeur that was seen as providing a model for all Spanish America (*Apristas* insisted upon calling the area Indo-America)? Or were they to be allowed material rewards vastly beyond what was required to satisfy their needs, thereby becoming for all practical purposes a new dominant culture? This is not made clear by the ideologists of the early APRA.

The challenge of APRA in the 1920s came to naught because of government repression and because the Peruvian middle sectors were not, in general, alienated from Leguía's *patria nueva*. Enjoying advantages and chances for advancement scarcely dreamt of previously, their representative figures were little inclined to embark upon an ill-defined crusade to crush a system from which they were benefiting and from which they anticipated ever greater future benefits.

In the 1930s the situation changed. Peru's capitalism, crippled by the effects of the world-wide depression, seemed for a time to be failing the bourgeoisie. Almost at the beginning of the crisis Leguía fell before a *golpe* directed by Luis M. Sánchez Cerro, an astute military officer. Very soon a considerable element within the middle sectors threw its support behind APRA, as did many disaffected youths of upper-class origins. At a time of adversity, moreover, *Aprista* propaganda struck a more responsive chord among the urban working classes of coastal Peru, especially in the north.

44 President Luis M. Sánchez Cerro, the dashing *cholo* officer who led the *golpe* that toppled Augusto B. Leguía in 1930; honestly elected to the presidency at the end of the following year, his success in forestalling APRA's subsequent attempts to gain power through revolution led to his assassination in 1933.

For a period of sixteen months, beginning at the end of 1931, the situation remained critical. But the swarthy *cholo* (in Peru the term refers to a mestizo) Sánchez Cerro, a tough and resourceful president despite his frail appearance, enjoyed an even greater mass following than APRA's pale-complexioned Haya de la Torre, and eventually he defeated the *Aprista* challenge. In a period of virtual civil war, he successfully countered force and violence with yet more massive force and violence.

Sánchez Cerro fell before an assassin's bullets in 1933, and for the ensuing six years Óscar R. Benavides, a military officer of aristocratic bearing with good connections among the leading families, relied upon somewhat suaver techniques to suppress opposition by APRA. He was able to do so because of his success in carrying through a programme of economic recovery in some ways more remarkable than that engineered at about the same time in Chile by Arturo Alessandri and Gustavo Ross. Economic recovery enabled the military régime to revive government paternalism, initiated principally by Leguía, and thereby to pacify the working classes. At the same time, economic recovery quieted the revolutionary ardour of the middle sectors, for many of whose members the established system appeared to be functioning satisfactorily once more.

Responding to the changing national mood, APRA began in the late 1930s to abandon its revolutionary position in favour of a programme that amounted in effect to little more than a claim that *Apristas* could run the established order better than the government. The transformation of APRA, far more evident in the mid-1940s, bore striking testimony to the resumption by the middle sectors of their traditional role as allies, even if reluctant ones, of the upper classes.

Relying upon an economic boom created by the high prices for Peruvian exports during the Second World War, Manuel Prado y Ugarteche, the scion of one of Lima's most aristocratic families, proved an adept political tactician and contrived even to gain the tacit support of APRA, still officially suppressed. Social, economic and political life functioned smoothly in Peru under his leadership as president between 1939 and 1945. But peaceful conditions did not last. Between 1945 and 1948 the unbridled political ambitions of the *Apristas*, on the one hand, and the long-standing military aversion to APRA, on the other – an aversion that many officers sought to justify by accusing Haya de la Torre of homosexuality – posed a threat to constitutional stability, though certainly not to the continuity of the established social order. The outcome was the military dictatorship of Manuel Odría from 1948 to 1956.

Odría, a Brigadier-General from the Andean town of Tarma with an avid interest in horse-racing, managed to maintain and even to strengthen the system that Leguía had forged in the 1920s. He protected the interests of the aristocracy, provided new economic opportunities for the middle sectors (in the process apparently turning a blind eye to corruption), cooperated with foreign capital, and relied upon revenues derived from taxing foreign enterprises and from the rise in export prices at the time of the Korean War to pour increasing sums of money into the social projects by means of which he gained a long enduring popularity among the country's urban poor. In the latter undertaking he was enormously aided by his wife. María Delgado de Odría presided over an expensive programme for distributing Christmas gifts to the children of poor families and dispensed charity on a lavish scale through a Centre of Social Assistance that bore her name.

The military dictatorship ended with an election in 1956 that brought Manuel Prado to his second term of office as constitutional president. This time Prado, diminutive, dapper and cunning, found the task of governing considerably more difficult than between 1939 and 1945. Perhaps his most remarkable accomplishment during his second term of office was to secure from the Vatican the annulment of his marriage, enabling him to marry a glamorous member of the country's high society. Affairs of state he found more difficult to manipulate, because the expedients devised earlier in the century for the purpose of avoiding basic change were ceasing to function effectively and beginning to develop internal strains. The challenge to the traditional society resulting from this situation and the response of the Peruvian military to it will be discussed briefly in the penultimate chapter.

Before turning to events after Prado's fall from power in 1962, it is necessary to consider the course of events in Argentina and Colombia. There we are confronted by a situation different from those examined so far. Both in Argentina and in Colombia the opening stages of social revolution actually took place. But in both countries the beneficiaries of the established order replied by force and succeeded in restoring the pre-revolutionary *status quo*. Here, as a result, the traditional society gained a reprieve through the failure of social revolution, with the result that it was possible, at least in the short term, to maintain the fundamental features of the old order without – as occurred elsewhere – having to introduce significant modifications.

45, 46 An extensive rail network and a booming wheat industry were indications of Argentina's stability and prosperity at the start of the twentieth century.

10 Aborted Revolution and a Reprieve for the Traditional Society i: The Case of Argentina

Progress towards economic development was the primary source of Argentinian national pride at the outset of the twentieth century. With the best railroad system in South America, with an economy solidly based on beef and wheat and with some striking advances towards industrialization already realized, Argentina had recovered from the depression of the early 1890s and was beginning to advance beyond the notable achievements of the fabled *ochenta* of the 1880s. In 1910 the republic, having recently constructed or rebuilt major portions of the capital city of Buenos Aires, celebrated the first centenary of the independence movement, and its leaders had the chance to point out the evidence of progress to an imposing array of foreign visitors. In their exuberant optimism the Argentinians seemed not totally unconvincing to some at least of their visitors when they assured them that their young republic would in the not too distant future rival the United States in economic development.

Many of those who set foot in Argentina for the first time in the early 1900s commented upon the undisguised materialism of the country's ruling class. To this materialism, manifested in part by a passionate, almost exclusive concern with national economic development, they attributed much of the country's progress. By no means all contemporary observers, however, were so approving. The Spanish philosopher José Ortega y Gasset expressed some rather serious misgivings. In an article written in 1924, Ortega speculated whether the spiritual shortcomings of Argentinians, their excessive covetousness and craving for creature comforts and their lack of a 'Seneca-like discipline' might not in the final analysis prevent the republic from ever attaining a place of honour among the nations of the world.

Visitors to Argentina at the turn of the century were invariably struck not only by the country's economic progress and its pervasive materialism but also by the number of immigrants. Largely as a result of immigration, the population had climbed from 1·8 million in 1869 to 7·8 million in 1914. In the period 1900–10, 30 per cent of all the people in Argentina were foreign born, compared to 14 per cent in the United States. Just as some observers were dubious about the ultimate consequences of unrestrained materialism, others entertained serious reservations about the long-term effects of immigration. For example, the Spanish philosopher Miguel de Unamuno contended, in an essay written in 1907, that Argentinians had been unable to assimilate either their foreign immigrants or the alien ideologies they brought with them. As a result, Unamuno maintained, Argentina lacked a collective spirit and was incapable of attaining the degree of integration and unification necessary to emerge as a true nation-state.

By the 1920s many Argentinians were ready to agree with Unamuno that immigration did not constitute an unmixed blessing. Leopoldo Lugones, perhaps the most eminent literary figure in Argentina at that time, wrote in 1930: 'The beggars, those who abandon and exploit children, the pimps, the pedlars of dangerous drugs and pornographic materials, the alcoholics, the vagrants and the professional agitators are, in the great majority, foreigners. There is reason to believe that their native countries purposely exported them to our land.' The most damaging vice that Lugones attributed to immigrants was the materialism with which they had allegedly perverted the country.

Lugones ascribed the encouragement that successive Argentinian governments, beginning in the early 1860s, had given to immigration to the influence of nineteenth-century liberalism, with its emphasis on material development and its dedication to destroying the corporative bastions of traditional society. And he blamed Argentinian bureaucracy, with its continuing infatuation with liberal values, for failing to take adequate steps to protect the land against the menace of immigrants.

Lugones' diagnosis reveals that the young republic was suffering a crisis of identity. Some Argentinians, those attacked by Lugones, endorsed the values of liberalism, advocated a *laissez-faire* approach to economics and politics that would stimulate individualism, and favoured a non-compartmentalized society from which corporate associations, whose legal existence was recognized by the state, had been eliminated. Others extolled the virtues of Hispanic traditions, championed government intervention in economic and social affairs, and advocated a hierarchically structured society within which a wide range of subsidiary corporations would enjoy privileges and assume responsibilities appropriate to their functions in national life.

Even in the early years of the twentieth century many Argentinians, among them Manuel Gálvez, had taken a stand against liberalism and positivism. Like Ortega y Gasset later, they were alarmed by their country's rampant materialism. Anticipating the views expressed by Lugones in 1930, they attributed the contamination of national culture by materialistic values to foreign immigrants, tending to make them the scapegoat for the country's ills, particularly for the newly emerging social problems. Foreign agitators were blamed for undermining social solidarity; and the materialism of the lower classes, allegedly the result of their penetration by immigrants, was held accountable for the enthusiasm with which they responded to subversive demagogues.

Alarmed by the growing strength of socialism and anarchism among the lower classes and by the threat, real or imagined, of social revolution, Gálvez and his associates spoke of the need to spiritualize Argentina by reanimating its traditional Catholic faith and its Hispanic social values; thereby the foreign immigrants could be absorbed into the true Argentinian culture. This was the basic theme that Gálvez developed in 1913 in his influential book, *El solar de la raza*. For Gálvez and his followers, spiritualization meant rendering the upper classes less greedy and less exploitative and more inclined to accept charitable obligations towards the lower classes. It also entailed curbing the desire of the masses for independent economic power and persuading them to seek moral rather than tangible rewards. The overall objective was to lead the masses back towards that dependence upon the paternalism of the classes above them that had supposedly obtained during a golden period in the past, before the arrival of immigrant hordes with anti-national, liberal values.

Catholic ideologists of the Gálvez school were unable to gain political power and thus did not have the opportunity to apply their prescriptions for resolving social problems. Instead political fortune favoured Hipólito Yrigoyen and his largely middle-sector followers in the Radical Party (Unión Cívica Radical). To them fell the task of seeking the means of mitigating social tensions so as to preserve the *status quo*.

A masterly political organizer, Yrigoyen triumphed in the presidential election of 1916. A lifelong bachelor, he was something of a Don Juan; but in most other respects this taciturn politician of Basque origins led an austere ascetic life. From his youth he had been profoundly influenced by the Krausist social philosophy that flourished in late nineteenth-century Spain. In line with Krausist views, he was anti-clerical and opposed to the Church's temporal influence. At the same time, he viewed with alarm the materialism of the masses, which he regarded as a threat to the established order. Undoubtedly his vaunted anti-Yankeeism sprang in part from his desire to prevent the individualistic materialism regarded as an inevitable product of United States culture from spreading among the Argentinian masses. As a Krausist, Yrigoyen assumed that individualism would necessarily unleash a revolutionary reaction against the sort of social structure that had traditionally existed in Spanish America.

Basically, Yrigoyen's aim was to realize the substantial benefits of liberalism while at the same time minimizing the egalitarian, levelling tendencies

47 *Peronista* propaganda condemning society's parasites 'who live without producing' and fostering working-class nationalism: at 'Our Theatre' the movie *Gangsters* is playing, while loyal and virtuous citizens eagerly arrive for work at the 'New Argentina' Factory.

that so many Spanish Americans regarded as inseparable from a liberal ideology. To accomplish his purposes, he had to be as insistent as Catholic conservatives upon curbing the materialism of the masses. At the same time, Yrigoyen, supported by the bourgeoisie and himself the offspring of a bourgeois family, wished to allow a fairly free rein to the material interests of the country's upper and middle classes and in this way to provide a stimulus for the economic development that was more important to him and his supporters than to the spokesmen of conservative Catholicism. In the final analysis he was searching for a synthesis between liberalism and traditionalism as the basis for resolving the social problem, and some of the same aspirations that guided him, consciously or subconsciously, would at a later date animate Juan Domingo Perón.

Disinclined by ideology and social prejudice to allow the masses genuine power within the political structure, Yrigoyen predictably moved towards the violent suppression of a series of labour strikes. Just as predictably, he sought to establish a new and comprehensive system of paternalistic government which, by extending services and fringe benefits to the lower classes, largely through state controlled labour unions, would win the support of the masses while at the same time reducing them to dependence upon the state.

Yrigoyen's major accomplishment was to defuse a potentially revolutionary situation by assembling a relatively smoothly functioning apparatus of government paternalism. At the same time various social projects inaugurated under the auspices of newly formed Catholic Action groups contributed to the social objectives of the régime, even though Yrigoyen, unlike Leguía in Peru, gave them no official backing. Some indices of economic development in the 1920s did not rise on a scale comparable to the 1880s or the first decade of the twentieth century, but there was greater social stability, and this is what seemed vitally important to the majority of the country's leaders.

While the masses were being won back to the established order, the social divisions among the ruling classes were being reduced. The 1920s, especially the period between 1922 and 1928 when Marcelo T. de Alvear served as president and abandoned the intransigent hostility that had characterized Yrigoyen's relations with all those outside his own party, witnessed a *rapprochement* between the largely middle-sector Unión Cívica Radical and the party of the landowning aristocracy, the Partido Autonomista Nacionalista (PAN). Unity among the privileged sections of society, towards which PAN leaders Carlos Pellegrini and Roque Saenz Peña had begun to work at the beginning of the century, now appeared close to reality. Middle-sector and upper-class interests became more and more intertwined through economic partnerships and political alliances, and sometimes through marriage as well. At the same time expanding opportunities for university education, beginning with the University Reform movement of 1918 in the interior city of Córdoba, provided an increasing segment of the middle sectors with the means of upward social mobility, enabling its members to acquire the qualifications that assured entry into the mushrooming bureaucracy and professional services.

But a new crisis emerged in the 1930s, a consequence in part of the world-wide economic depression. At the beginning of that decade a new rift developed in the ranks of the ruling classes – an augury of a situation that was to appear in several other Spanish American republics only in the 1950s and 1960s – as a military *coup* brought an end to Radical rule and re-installed in power a traditional ranching aristocracy whose members depended on the export trade for their economic well-being. The privileges of bourgeois groups, numerically more formidable than elsewhere in Spanish America because of Argentina's higher rate of industrialization, were sharply curtailed, and these groups began to attribute all the nation's problems to the selfishness of landowners who had allegedly sold out the country's interests to the foreign capitalists who controlled the export markets. A representative figure of the alienated bourgeoisie was Raúl Scalabrini Ortiz. In his widely influential writings Scalabrini drew attention to the fact that in the mid-1930s approximately 50 per cent of the country's industrial capital was in foreign hands. He claimed in addition that, of the country's 50 billion pesos of national wealth, only 18·46 billion pesos were in Argentinian hands, and he blamed this upon the lack of concern of the *vendepatria* élite with overall national development.

Commenting upon these circumstances, Mark Falcoff, in an article written in 1972, noted that a 'trickle-down' effect had benefited the bourgeois groups during the late nineteenth and early twentieth centuries, and that as a consequence its members had been willing to remain 'in the shadow of Argentina's traditional élite'. In the adverse period of the 1930s, however, that élite concerned itself exclusively with its own interests. No longer benefiting from a 'trickle-down', the bourgeoisie spawned a number of spokesmen who began to challenge the upper classes they had once defended. However aggrieved they might feel towards those above them in social prominence and political power, the emergent Argentinian nationalistic bourgeoisie could not find a common ground with the urban labourers whose radical social doctrines they feared and abhorred.

The increased difficulty that the state encountered in raising the revenue necessary to maintain its various social projects contributed in another way to the crisis precipitated by the depression. At the same time an unprecedented number of labourers from the rural provinces began to flock into Buenos Aires and other major cities, offsetting a drastic decline in immigration that might otherwise have imperilled urban economic enterprises, but also throwing an additional burden upon the social services. The native migrants, economically less resourceful than many of the foreign labourers of the preceding era, suffered serious exploitation in an urban environment to which they were unaccustomed. The situation was exacerbated by the contempt of the light-skinned upper-classes, particularly in Buenos Aires,

48 Juan Domingo Perón with his second wife, Eva. Though *peronismo* has retained its original appeal, Perón's brief return to Buenos Aires in 1972, after seventeen years in Spain, indicated that 'El Líder' still dominated the movement he founded.

for the newly arrived, darker-skinned mestizos from the interior, whom they disparagingly referred to as *los cabecitas negras* (the little black heads). Eventually the *cabecitas negras*, mingling with an old-line urban labour force and with them coming collectively to be known as the *descamisados* (shirtless ones), were to find their champions in Juan and Eva Perón, as indeed, at least initially, would many of the bourgeois nationalists.

Argentinian statesmen and intellectuals in the mid-1930s were obsessed with their country's imagined rendezvous with destiny, and this was another factor in contributing to heightened social instability and a new challenge to the traditional society. Under the leadership of foreign minister Carlos Saavedra Lamas, they began to dream of challenging the United States for hegemony in the affairs of the hemisphere. But it was obvious that national greatness could not be attained unless the country succeeded in pushing forward its economic development on a scale matching and even surpassing that of the *ochenta*. This meant assimilating the masses into the economy by inducing them to be more productive and acquire the purchasing power necessary to provide an adequate internal market for the products of an expanding economy.

Since it was no longer possible to rely upon European immigrants to supply a labour force with a capitalist mentality, fulfilment of the country's destiny seemed to depend upon creating a profit-motivated and perhaps even to some degree economically self-reliant lower class out of the country's native masses. But a profit-motivated and economically self-reliant lower class meant the end of a sub-culture resigned to dependence upon the largesse of the privileged few; it meant, as spokesmen of conservative,

Catholic, traditionalist Argentina began to warn with intensified stridency, nothing less than social revolution. The problem was how to assure economic development, upon which dreams of national greatness rested, while at the same time avoiding social revolution. Here was the dilemma that a new generation of Argentinian leaders confronted.

Juan Domingo Perón professed to have found the answer. The name he gave to his administration's highly eclectic ideology was *justicialismo*. Just past his fiftieth birthday when he garnered 56 per cent of the vote in the 1946 presidential election, Perón divided his private time largely between amours and motor cycles. A career officer in the army who seemed to exude *joie de vivre* and virility, he had served as military attaché in Chile – he was thrown out of that country in 1938 when caught in an attempt to steal its national defence plans – and in Italy. Just before becoming president he had married Eva Duarte, a slender blonde of striking appearance well known in Buenos Aires as a radio actress – malicious gossip spoke of other and less respectable activities, but without any real evidence. She became one of the principal propagandists of *justicialismo*, which included among its many sources of inspiration both Catholic social theoreticians and Krausist *pensadores*.

The attraction of *justicialismo*, according to its proponents, was that it supplied the requisite formulae for blending in proper proportions materialism and individualism, spirituality and collectivism. Quite clearly the hope of many upper-class Argentinians was that the materialism of the masses, to be nourished to some degree by allowing them more purchasing power through increases in real wages, could be contained by educating them also to recognize the importance of inward fulfilment. At first Perón turned to the Catholic Church to help furnish the masses with spiritual contentment. Then, from 1951 onwards, he relied increasingly upon a highly emotional and secular nationalism.

If the masses were not to pose a revolutionary threat, their individualism also had to be curbed. Instead of seeking individual advancement, they had to be induced to seek realization and satisfaction within various collective bodies which depended upon the state for the security and advantage of their members. Advancing far beyond previous measures, Perón organized the urban lower classes into government controlled labour associations which served as intermediaries through which the state bestowed fringe benefits upon workers.

Justicialismo posited four basic elements in human existence. A delicate balance between these elements was essential for the success of Perón's policies and the preservation of a two-culture society. Among the lower classes, spirituality and collectivism would have to take preponderance over, without eliminating, material gain and individual initiative. Among the

49 During her life a magnetic propagandist who inspired tremendous popular support for her husband's policies, Eva de Perón remains a living legend twenty years after her death, adored by some Argentinians who seriously seek her canonization and just as passionately reviled by others.

upper and middle sectors, materialism and individual initiative would have to predominate, but not to the exclusion of the non-material satisfactions afforded by spirituality and collectivism. This balance was never achieved by the *Peronistas* and their failure led to the eventual overthrow of their leader.

Economic problems paved the way for Perón's downfall, although this was not apparent for some time even to the dictator's harshest critics. At first, the administration found it deceptively easy to pay the formidable bills accumulating from its social programmes. The government could, for example, force landowners to sell agricultural products to it at reduced prices, and then dispose of them to foreign purchasers at the inflated international prices of post Second World War days. The initial ease with which he funded his policies led Perón to write a revealing letter to his friend across the Andes, Carlos Ibáñcz, who was elected president of Chile in 1952. The letter was reproduced in 1953 in the book *Nuestros vecinos justicialistas* by the Chilean author Alejandro Magnet and part of it reads:

My Friend: Give to the people, especially to the workers, all that is possible. When it seems to you that you are giving them too much, give them more. You will see the results. Everyone will try to scare you with the spectre of an economic collapse. But all of this is a lie. There is nothing more elastic than the economy which everyone fears so much because no one understands it.

He was deceiving himself. The victim of his own economic naivety, by 1953 Perón faced an economic collapse. International prices for Argentinian exports had fallen to more normal levels and landowners, frustrated by the unfair selling conditions imposed by the government, had responded by reducing production. A succession of drought years made matters worse. The huge sterling reserves accumulated in England during the war had been squandered in purchasing a rundown railroad system from British capitalists. And public funds had been lavished on various ill-conceived industrialization projects aimed more at indulging national pride and enriching a few friends of the administration than at contributing to balanced, integrated economic development. Desperately in need of money, the president jeopardized his support among Argentinian nationalists by toning down if not abandoning the anti-Yankeeism which had been a prominent feature of early *peronismo*. He opened Argentinian oilfields to United States investors on generous terms and in exchange received a sizable loan from Washington. Despite this, the economy continued to deteriorate.

Because of the economic crisis, Perón's administration could no longer maintain the rewards to which workers had become accustomed. The president was further handicapped by the loss of his wife, who died of cancer in 1952. In some ways a more charismatic propagandist than Perón himself, and just possibly more genuinely compassionate, Eva had been able to explain the purposes and goals of *justicialismo* to the masses in a manner that made them feel important and convinced them that the government had their interests at heart. In her ability to impart a sense of dignity to the lower classes through the rhetoric of nationalism, Eva Duarte de Perón has had few peers in the history of Spanish America.

Unable, as circumstances worsened, to provide the customary rewards to the lower classes, Perón faced a situation more and more fraught with the perils of social revolution. Increasingly rebellious voices, many of them belonging to alienated members of the upper and middle classes, began to demand that the possessions of the rich be expropriated in order to finance the better life that workers had savoured in the halcyon days of *peronismo*. The aim of the revolutionaries was to force the moneyed interests to relinquish the power and privileges accruing to them through wealth.

Perón had come to office determined to preserve the established order by introducing certain minimal changes and modifications. By August 1955, when his position was desperate, he decided that his only hope of remaining in power lay in placing himself at the head of a social revolution. On the last day of the month he delivered a fiery demagogic speech, demanding confiscation of the wealth of the upper and middle classes and proclaiming the distribution of arms to the lower classes so that they might assure the success of the revolution. The president's uncharacteristic clarion call to revolution crystallized and focused the uncoordinated opposition long dormant among the military, the Church and the privileged classes in general. Before September had passed, Perón was in exile.

A reluctant revolutionary but avid for personal power at any price, Perón had brought his country to the very brink and even into the early stages of a major social upheaval. As it turned out, the social revolution was aborted. Dissident elements were systematically crushed by the reactionary conservative elements that gained the upper hand within the armed forces upon the dictator's downfall, and Argentina returned to a *status quo* that antedated in some respects the whole Perón era.

In the post-Perón years *peronismo* refused to die, despite many attempts at its repression. Perhaps the Argentinian left-wing intellectual Juan José Sebreli put his finger on one of the important reasons when he wrote:

> The ten years of *peronismo* signified, in sum, a challenge to the rule of custom, the majesty of established values, of all the moral clichés and morbid inhibitions of philistinism, of ideological hypocrisy. . . . Perón seems, in his later years [of rule], to have conceived a theory according to which all of humanity, himself included, had to have fun. . . . *Peronismo* demonstrated that it is possible to combine the most unrestricted liberty with despotism.

Since the fall of Perón, Argentinians have had little to amuse themselves about. This, rather than its ideological attractions or even the stagnant economic situation, could be a reason for *peronismo*'s lingering support. In the premium that he encouraged Argentinians to place upon amusement, Perón may have stumbled on to a highly significant non-material reward.

After the fall of Perón, Argentine society was plagued by the longing of many of its leaders to return to an era in which the masses, the detested *cabecitas negras*, could not lay claim to a status of dignity and importance. Social tensions continued unresolved, and against this background the various components within a restored oligarchy have manœuvred towards a political stalemate. Large landowners, industrialists, the army, the Church, the professional classes and intellectuals, as well as organized labour, all seem interested only in pursuing group privileges and intransigently refuse to assume burdens in the common interest.

The most populous republic of Spanish America – its population in the mid-1960s was 23 million – Argentina after the fall of Perón was in a period of drifting and stagnation. The decade 1955–65 witnessed a regressive redistribution of income, and the increase in per capita productivity, averaging 0·5 per cent annually, was one of the lowest in the world. The plight of Argentina was evidence that political leaders are apt to be most reactionary and blind in the years immediately following an aborted social revolution. This conclusion is confirmed by events in Colombia at approximately the same period.

50 The pillars of the conservative Colombian *oligarquía* are satirized in this painting by Fernando Botero, *The Presidential Family*, which includes a general and a bishop.

11 Aborted Revolution and a Reprieve for the Traditional Society ii: The Case of Colombia

The élite in Colombia has demonstrated at least a minimal degree of flexibility, relieving social pressures at crucial times by absorbing potential dissidents from the middle ranks of society. To a greater extent than in most other Spanish American republics, however, the composition of the *oligarquía*, many of whose members take pride in tracing their ancestry back to the colonial aristocracy, has remained frozen. In this respect, Colombia affords a striking contrast to neighbouring Venezuela.

In Bogotá, Colombia's highland capital, a tightly-knit ruling clique has looked down with disdain upon the dark-skinned coastal dwellers, among whom the presence of African slaves in colonial times has left an indelible mark. The Bogotano élite has tended also to exhibit open contempt for the large mestizo populace found not only in the capital but in most interior cities. Unlike Caracas, Bogotá, at least on the upper levels of society, has not become a racial, social and regional melting pot.

By the middle of the nineteenth century, the two great political parties, Conservative and Liberal, both of them largely but not exclusively aristocratic in their early leadership, had come into being. Rivalry between them resulted from family feuds, personal antagonisms, regional animosities, as well as from economic and social friction reaching back at least to the middle of the eighteenth century. Ideological questions also contributed to Conservative-Liberal discord – though not nearly to the extent implied by the Peruvian writer Francisco García Calderón's comment on Colombia's bloody civil wars: 'The truth is saved but Colombia perishes.'

The pro-clerical Conservatives, who in general advocated a strong, active role for the Catholic Church in temporal affairs, saw in liberalism the inevitable fruit of the Protestant heresy which, in their view, consisted essentially of exalting the individual conscience. In social and economic matters this heresy manifested itself in the rampant individualism of liberalism, leading to exploitation of the masses, and this in turn, Conservatives maintained, was bound to give rise, as supposedly the only effective remedy, to atheistic, materialistic socialism. Conservatives favoured a corporative structure, in which the people would participate in society through municipal, regional, class and functional groups, with rights and obligations conferred upon them not as equal members of a single unstratified society but rather as members of specific subsidiary organisms. In the Conservative view the corporative structure would safeguard the social hierarchies that atomistic individualism threatened with extinction. As a further safeguard, Conservatives stressed the need for Church and state to collaborate in paternalistic programmes that assured material security for the lower classes. In addition, they hoped that subsidiary, corporative groups would develop their own internal charitable organizations in which the more affluent members would care for the indigent.

Liberals, on the other hand, desired a secular society free from Church influence. In the name of individual liberty, they advocated suppression of all those intermediate organizations that in a corporative structure had divided society into different compartments and had defined the rights and duties of citizens in terms of the particular subsidiary group to which they belonged. Taking much of their economics from Adam Smith and David Ricardo, Liberals saw little if any need for social or economic intervention by the state.

Colombia's Liberals dominated the political scene, with occasional interruptions, between 1849 and 1880. In line with their anti-corporative, individualist credo, they attacked such privileged corporations as the military and the Church, depriving the latter of much of its landed property. They also dissolved the communal landholdings of Indian villages, ostensibly in order to introduce the natives to the benefits of private landownership. In actual practice, as in contemporary Mexico and other Spanish American republics, it was the wealthy classes rather than the poverty-stricken natives who ultimately gained possession of the property expropriated from Indian *comunidades* and reservations (*resguardos*).

No longer cared for paternalistically, as they had been on lands owned by the Church, many rural peasants migrated into Colombia's numerous urban centres, where they were joined by Indians deprived of their livelihood as their villages and reservations suffered confiscation. In the cities, however, employment opportunities were minimal, partly because a once-flourishing small-scale industry had been virtually wiped out by the liberal assault on tariffs. As economic distress generated dangerous discontent among the lower classes and middle sectors, many influential Colombians who had approved the confiscation of Church properties reacted with dismay when the Liberal government moved to abolish religious instruction in all schools.

This was the troubled situation when Rafael Núñez came to power in 1880. At first this poet-politician hoped to form a coalition of Independents and Liberals. Some of the country's more intransigent Liberals, grouped together in the Olimpo Radical, promptly sought to overthrow the new president. Núñez triumphed in the ensuing civil war, but only at the price of surrendering political independence. By the mid-1880s Núñez, who was to dominate Colombian politics until his death in 1894, had come to rely almost exclusively on Conservative Party support.

The Conservative restoration brought the Church a return of its privileges and much of its wealth. Secure once more as a powerful landholding institution, it also gained firmer control over the entire educational system than it had enjoyed since colonial times. Enjoying once again a large and steady income, it resumed its charitable programmes that had been interrupted during the period of Liberal ascendancy. The Conservative restoration also resulted in the protection of Indians against further loss of land. Moreover, tariffs were reimposed and the government facilitated the formation of various monopolistic business enterprises that vastly aided middle-sector entrepreneurs. In short, Colombia – at the very time when liberalism, feeding upon an influx of immigrants, was triumphant in Argentina – returned in some fair measure to a corporative orientation, while at the same time the government, in the interest of preserving social solidarity, pursued a policy of intervention in economic affairs.

In the early twentieth century, especially during the five-year rule of Rafael Reyes (1904–09), Conservatives and Liberals, sharing a sense of humiliation over the loss of Panama in 1903 – largely the work of the Roosevelt administration in the United States – began to forge the basis of a *modus vivendi*. Reyes, moreover, was a man who would not put up with nonsense, a fact he demonstrated when he helped ride down and then oversaw the summary execution of some would-be assassins who had somehow managed to miss him in the fusillade they fired into the presidential carriage. Continuation of the Conservative-Liberal feud struck Reyes as nonsensical, and he exerted whatever additional pressure was required to persuade representatives of both parties to collaborate in serving his administration. An arrangement was devised by which the Liberals promised not to vote, so as to spare the incumbent Conservatives embarrassment at election time, in exchange for which they were granted many important appointments and offices and an increased share in decision-making at the national level. Once more enjoying some measure of political power and secure in the possession of their wealth, the Liberals co-operated in preserving the established order. A situation was already developing which would later prompt the quip that the principal difference between the once bitterly antagonistic parties was that the Liberals drank in public and prayed in private, while Conservatives drank in private and prayed in public.

Political reconciliation was followed by social accommodation as a new generation of Colombian leaders known as the Generation of 1910 climbed into the saddle. Among the Liberals once associated with the Olimpo

Radical, whose membership was mainly drawn from the merchant and business class, a number made their peace with the political system and then married into aristocratic families. Once they had thus assured their position within the old seignioral régime, bourgeois Liberals no longer desired to destroy it.

The new harmony among the Colombian upper classes was undoubtedly facilitated by the increased tempo of economic development from which the country benefited at the beginning of the century. At this time coffee became the major export crop – produced then, as it has been ever since, by a large number of relatively small estate-owners whose individual economic power was not adequate to guarantee them a high position within the ruling *oligarquía*. Banana production also offered promising possibilities and in 1912 the United Fruit Company extended its operations into Colombia. Cattle-raising, sugar and the textile industry – which, like coffee but unlike bananas, remained in the hands of native capitalists – also contributed to prosperity. Economic dislocations caused by the First World War temporarily slowed the rate of development; but in the 1920s it began to assume almost runaway proportions. In this period of the 'Dance of the Millions', some important petroleum resources were signed away on a temporary basis to foreign firms, but other resources remained under national control. The same sort of prosperity – although less dependent than elsewhere on foreign capital – that had helped Juan Vicente Gómez to consolidate his hold on Venezuela, enabled Uruguay to finance the expanding system of social services inaugurated by Batlle y Ordóñez, permitted Carlos Ibáñez to assemble the machinery of a new paternalism in Chile and allowed Augusto B. Leguía to introduce the wonders of the *patria nueva* in Peru, now strengthened the position of Colombia's Conservative-Liberal alliance. The alliance seemed so secure that in 1930, when the Liberals, taking advantage of a Conservative split, abandoned the old agreement to refrain from voting and actually elected their candidate, there followed a completely peaceful transfer of political power.

Beneath the surface, however, ominous signs of discord had appeared. In Colombia the government took relatively little advantage of the new prosperity to overhaul and expand the social services, perhaps because its fruits went more to native than to foreign capitalists and thus were not tapped by taxation. Hoping that the Church would, through its large-scale charitable undertakings and its monopolistic control of the educational system, impart to the masses a due respect for the virtue of resignation, the upper classes largely ignored the fact that the Church also preached denial for men of wealth, exhorting them to devote some of their profits to the maintenance of social justice. Strikes, student agitation and even labour violence became increasingly commonplace in the 1920s. In 1925 a group of

Colombians founded the country's first Communist Party. Three years later a major incident shook the country. Workers and landless peasants seized some unused property in the coastal area of Santa Marta which the government had set aside for the United Fruit Company. The violence that followed, as the military, on government orders, ousted the squatters resulted in at least one hundred fatal casualties – some estimates ran a great deal higher.

Since the time of Núñez successive Colombian governments had tacitly permitted the occupation of unused land, even though it was privately owned; if squatters lived on the land for a stipulated period and made some improvements, it eventually became theirs. This practice provided a safety valve for social pressures roughly similar to the homestead law in the United States. But in 1928 it appeared that the safety valve had been closed. Outrage and consternation spread among Colombia's poorer classes who, because newspapers were now being delivered by air to once isolated areas, quickly learned of what had transpired at Santa Marta.

In denouncing the massacre and helping to organize a congressional investigation, a young member of the Liberal Party, Jorge Eliécer Gaitán, rapidly rose to national prominence and acquired a large popular following. Gaitán is a controversial figure; but if his speeches and writings are taken at face value, it would appear that what he desired was the transformation of Colombia into a pluralistic society, in which various social and functional groups could rely upon their own strength and independent bargaining power to demand of society what they considered their due. Such views were a direct threat to all that was most sacrosanct within the traditional society. By his contention that the conscience of the upper classes could no longer be relied upon and that social justice must be based upon the power of those below rather than the charity of those above, Gaitán created a serious division within the ranks of the privileged classes, which had remained fairly well united since the *modus vivendi* of the early years of the century.

The threat from the Left to the unity of the Colombian ruling class was matched by one from the Right. Within the Conservative Party an increasingly vociferous faction emerged led by Laureano Gómez, owner of the Bogotá daily newspaper *El Siglo*, which appeared to consider its interpretations of Catholic doctrine more authoritative and binding than those of the Vatican and the Colombian episcopacy. Gómez and his followers, the so-called *Laureanistas*, saw the new social crisis through the eyes of nineteenth-century Catholic Conservatives. In their view Colombia's troubles stemmed from the liberal heresy, based on exalted individualism, which led allegedly to the reaction of atheistic Communism. According to Gómez, many of his associates within the Conservative Party had been contaminated by contact with the heretical, secular-minded, materialistic Liberals, whose sins were compounded by their Masonic affiliations. In this way they had fallen into the false liberal assumption that the social problem could be solved by material means alone, simply by ministering to the physical needs of the masses. Such a solution, Gómez and the *Laureanistas* warned, would inevitably fail. The result would simply be to arouse the insatiable appetites of the lower orders and lead to a levelling social revolution, control over which would undoubtedly be captured by Marxists.

In the view of the *Laureanistas*, the answer to Colombia's problems lay in spiritualizing the country through the traditional Catholic faith. This entailed reawakening in the upper classes the belief that celestial rewards awaited those who practised charity and in impressing upon the masses the truth that their task in this life was to prepare, through Christian resignation, for the next world. Although not all churchmen agreed with his prescriptions, Gómez insisted that social services and paternalistic programmes should be carried out not by the civil service, which was likely to remain corrupted for some time to come by liberalism and materialism, but by the Church, which alone could instil the spiritual values without which the social problem was insoluble.

Gómez and his followers also postulated a major social and political transformation in the countryside. In their view, the rural masses, dependent in many instances upon the paternalism of local Liberal *caudillos* (bosses), should transfer their allegiance instead to local collective and co-operative associations, to which they would be assigned under the leadership of the clergy – thereby achieving one of the long-held objectives of Catholic Action. A variety of social services would then be channelled through these associations to their members. In this way the detested Liberal Party would be crushed in its old rural strongholds. At the same time, rural society would be reconstructed on a corporative basis, with the Church providing spiritual guidance to each of the subsidiary groups. In the countryside, in short, would begin the movement to end the foolish experiment with parliamentary democracy, which, according to the *Laureanistas*, was discredited throughout the world.

Neither Gaitán nor Gómez was content with the middle-of-the-road position of the majority of the Liberal-Conservative alliance. Each wished a major reconstruction of the social and political order. These differences, which splintered the ruling oligarchy, inevitably weakened the established system; the difficulties were multiplied because of the rigidity, even at mid-century, of Colombian society. The fact that upward social mobility was difficult, although not entirely impossible, bred discontent among the middle sectors, driving some of their members to support either Liberal or Conservative extremists, and impelling others to seek backers among the

51 Jorge Eliécer Gaitán, charismatic leader of one wing of the Colombian Liberal Party, whose assassination in April 1948 unleashed the full fury of *la violencia*, an era marked in its early stages by a savage rural revolt against established authority.

restless proletariat for their own revolutionary programmes.

The lower classes had ample reason for restlessness in the period immediately following the Second World War. By that time the ruling élite had lost interest in the social programmes introduced in the mid-1930s under the Liberal leader, Alfonso López Pumarejo. López himself felt constrained to resign in 1945 before completing his second term of office. He had insisted upon pushing ahead with government sponsored social programmes. But his mood had contrasted too sharply with that of the majority of Colombian political leaders who, reading the meaning that most appealed to them into the defeat of Germany, Italy and Japan, concluded that the concept of a managed economy had been discredited and that the future belonged to economic liberalism.

At this juncture Gaitán appeared to be in the best position to capitalize upon the discontent among the lower classes. He had concentrated his efforts for some time on establishing communication with the masses and instilling into the lowly born a sense of class consciousness and an awareness of the power which they could wield as a united and assertive force. For the first time in Colombian history he built up a political network that reached into some of the more remote rural areas as well as into the slums of most cities. In this way Gaitán sought to break down the regional and semi-corporative mentality of the masses that had led them in the past to think of themselves primarily as residents of a certain village, workers on a particular estate, members of a specific labour organization or backers of either one of the two major political parties. His message was that the deprived Colombian masses should think of themselves as members of one vast impoverished working class.

Nevertheless it was the Conservative Party, perhaps because it was less divided, that returned to power in 1946. Before long the new president, Mariano Ospina Pérez, gave indications of adopting the extremist position of Laureano Gómez, for he began to treat Liberals as evil men with whom no compromise was permissible. To forestall the possibility of a Liberal return to power, a possibility made all the more frightening by the prospect of Gaitán capturing control of the party, the government unleashed a programme of repression which marked the beginning of what came to be known as the era of *la violencia*. It was directed primarily against the bastions of Liberal strength in rural Colombia, but the government also harassed Liberal organizations in Bogotá and other cities.

In April 1948 Gaitán was assassinated, under circumstances that remain largely unexplained, and Bogotá erupted. In a few days of tumultuous rioting, vast areas of the city were looted and razed. Upon news of Gaitán's assassination the countryside also erupted. But with his death the elaborate network of communications he had built up between Bogotá and the other parts of the country collapsed overnight. His supporters in the countryside no longer had the means of making their power felt in the capital. In their anger and frustration, they lashed out indiscriminately against the nearest objects upon which they could vent their fury. Any Conservative landowner and his family, any local Conservative politician would do. Soon violence begot violence as government forces sought to terrorize the traditional centres of Liberal strength in the provinces into submission. In many regions, every semblance of law and order disappeared and violence became a way of life for those who chose to remain rather than flee for safety to the cities. In all, *la violencia* may have claimed some 200,000 lives – out of a population estimated in the 1960s at 18 million – in the period between 1947 and the mid-1960s. But the violence remained almost completely uncoordinated and without focus. Although arising largely out of discontent with the established system, it was never effectively directed against that system.

Colombia's *violencia* was in effect an aborted social revolution. Like Argentina, Colombia in the 1950s went through the initial stages of social revolution. In both instances, the revolution was defeated and the established order gained a reprieve.

Taking advantage of their reprieve, the Colombian ruling classes mended their ways to some degree, patched up their quarrels, silenced for a time at least the extremists within the Liberal and Conservative Parties, and – aided by mutual desire to overthrow military dictator Gustavo Rojas Pinilla (1953–57) whom neither party could claim or control – were able in 1958 to begin to implement an agreement by which the two parties were to share the presidency and other high offices alternately until 1974. Meanwhile, a few social palliatives – financed in part by funds contributed by the United States under the Alliance for Progress – were introduced, including an extremely tentative agrarian reform. Hoping to steal some of the populist thunder of Rojas Pinilla and his daughter María Eugenia, who enjoyed widespread support among the masses in the late 1960s and early

52 The body of Jorge Gaitán surrounded by a group of his followers.

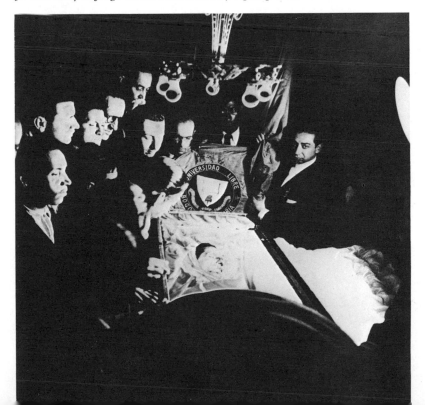

1970s, the government also threatened the moneyed classes with the possibility of taxation to help finance the country's essential social and development projects.

On the whole, however, Colombia's Liberal and Conservative politicians scarcely distinguished themselves by positive measures, any more than the reactionary civilian and military rulers of Argentina did in the fifteen years following Perón's overthrow. It is perhaps worth repeating that complacency seems to grip the leaders of countries that have just undergone aborted social revolutions. When passions and antagonisms are aroused to the point necessary to unleash revolution, and when that revolution is crushed and liquidated, considerable time must apparently elapse before a new revolutionary situation can develop.

Cuba underwent an aborted revolution at a much earlier date than Colombia, in the early and middle 1930s. The reprieve this gave to the leaders of the established system was not, however, as long as they had counted upon and time ran out at the end of the 1950s. Before we turn to the events that enabled Fidel Castro to oust Cuba's old guard leadership, it is, however, necessary to review briefly the main developments after the Second World War that posed new challenges to traditional society, not only in Cuba but throughout Spanish America.

12 Contemporary Spanish America: New Challenges to Tradition

In the aftermath of the Second World War, concepts of liberal, *laissez-faire* economics enjoyed a revival throughout much of Spanish America. Numerous political leaders and intellectuals assumed that the future belonged to the competitive, individualistic approach to economic questions thought to prevail in its purest form in the United States. Unfortunately they tended to see their model for future success in a highly distorted manner; for the economies of the United States and of the European powers that made the most rapid post-war recoveries were a good deal more managed than Spanish America's new generation of apologists for the unregulated market place liked to imagine.

In the years immediately following the Second World War, moreover, the Catholic Church, which some years earlier had enjoyed a resurgence of power as the social conscience of the upper classes and as the instigator of many paternalistic social services, entered into a new decline. One factor accounting for this was that in the 1920s and 1930s churchmen had tended to associate themselves with anti-democratic, corporative philosophies. After 1945 this contributed to a fresh wave of anti-clericalism whose spokesmen found it convenient to distort reality and to identify the social philosophy of Catholicism with Fascism. The Church, according to them, no longer deserved to be heeded because it had embraced the ideology of the vanquished Axis powers.

For these and other reasons, the upper classes were increasingly unwilling to assume moral obligations towards those below them on the social ladder. This change of attitude posed an ultimate threat to the paternalism to which Spanish American governments had turned early in the century as a means of appeasing social tensions. For a time, however, this fact was obscured by the ready availability of foreign capital. Immediately after the end of the war, Spanish America experienced a massive input of private capital investment from abroad. Later, capital became available from a number of new international lending agencies. Foreign loans and money collected through taxes on foreign enterprises allowed Spanish American governments to finance their programmes of social security and economic protection for the working classes.

By the late 1960s, however, a new situation had developed, symbolized by the collapse of the Alliance for Progress. Foreign capital was no longer so readily available. Foreign investors were alienated by what they considered to be excessive demands by Spanish American governments and feared the confiscation of their assets. The Spanish American moneyed classes resented the conditions imposed by foreign lenders. Each exacerbated the other, and the result was a rapid deterioration.

An important factor alienating the Spanish American upper classes and wounding their pride was the much advertised demand for internal reform imposed by the architects of the Alliance for Progress. The Alliance, launched by President John F. Kennedy at the outset of his presidential term in 1961, aimed at the improvement of conditions in Latin America through a ten-year allotment of 10 billion United States dollars, both public and private, to the republics to the south. Assignment of funds was to be dependent upon acceptance by Latin American leaders of social and economic reforms designed largely in Washington. Profoundly insensitive

53 President John F. Kennedy inaugurates a low-cost housing development in Colombia, one of the many projects financed during the 1960s by the Alliance for Progress. By the end of the decade its friends and foes alike agreed that the Alliance was dead and that Colombia, once billed as an Alliance showcase, had attained little progress.

to deep-seated cultural differences, the United States experts who shaped Alliance policies assumed that socio-economic measures judged appropriate to their own country would provide a panacea for problems south of the border. The Alliance was notable chiefly for arousing hopes in Latin America that could not be fulfilled and for alienating directing classes through demands for reform that were viewed, understandably, as a new type of United States intervention in internal affairs.

On the whole the upper classes of Spanish America had been content to accept dependence upon foreign capital – and even upon occasion to put up with considerable abuse from it – so long as no conditions of internal reform were attached by outsiders. When reforms were demanded as a condition for foreign loans, grants and investment they not unnaturally rebelled – thereby duplicating the actions of the internal sub-culture when the dominant culture has attempted to reform it. The result was to create in the later 1960s a climate that was not conducive to foreign investment, and the decline in funds from abroad meant a greater burden on the native capitalists, in so far as it now fell to them – if anyone – to provide the revenue necessary to maintain the level of social spending required to assure internal stability. It need hardly be said that this prospect was highly unwelcome, particularly since their commitment to economic liberalism predisposed the privileged classes against many features of paternalism and state intervention.

The dramatic population increases, averaging by the 1960s some 3 per cent a year – with the notable exceptions of Argentina and Uruguay where annual rises have been more in the region of 1·5 per cent – meant that the cost of providing for the needs of the masses soared. In 1900 there were approximately 61 million Latin Americans, Brazilians included. In 1967 the population for the twenty Latin American republics was estimated at some 250 million, including about 85 million Brazilians, and was projected at 600 million or higher for the year 2000. Furthermore, the percentage of the young within the population – that is, those not yet able to enter the productive sector of the economy – was steadily rising, thereby placing an ever larger burden upon the productive members of society. By the end of the 1960s the majority of the population in most Spanish American countries was under twenty years of age.

The magnitude of Spanish America's population problem becomes clear when we consider that, according to widely accepted analyses, a 9 per cent annual increase in capital investment is required to sustain a 3 per cent growth in per capita income. This is a sizable investment rate, but in a country where the population is expanding by 3 per cent a year it will, of course, only suffice to maintain the economic *status quo*. Furthermore, in any given period an increase in employment is likely to be only one-third of an increment in per capita income. Thus if a country's per capita income rises 6 per cent a year, a rate not consistently maintained by any of the Spanish American republics except Mexico and Venezuela, employment will climb by only 2 per cent. But in most Spanish American countries the annual population growth is well above 2 per cent. In consequence, rates of unemployment and underemployment assume runaway proportions, imposing constantly growing demands on hard-pressed governments for financing unemployment benefits, assistance and other social overheads.

In view of the imperative need for economic growth, many of the leading political and intellectual figures in Spanish America have begun to urge the overriding importance of making the masses economically productive by inculcating the values and knowledge that will make them an integrated part of an expanding capitalist society. These were the views of the late nineteenth-century positivist reformers, and they have been revived because it is felt that economic catastrophe can only be avoided by assimilating all elements of society into the world of capitalist development previously reserved for members of the dominant culture. But how can the sub-culture be assimilated into a productive, capitalist society without thereby destroying the established and traditional social order? This is the problem that challenges those in Spanish America concerned with development in the second half of the twentieth century, yet still dedicated to preserving the two-culture society. It is not a new problem within the context of the Hispanic world, but it is unique in the intensity it has acquired in recent years.

Even if the governing classes wished to continue to isolate the masses from individualistic, acquisitive, materialistic goals, they would find it increasingly difficult to do so, short of exercising totalitarian control over radio, television, the press and the entire educational system. At the present time the communications media and the schools, controlled essentially by men of the middle sectors within the dominant culture, are forcing bourgeois values upon the lower classes. Thus it has become far more difficult than ever before to sustain the segregated existence of two cultures, of *dos repúblicas*, upon which the preservation of the traditional society has largely depended since colonial times.

In the wake of the population problem, the family – another base upon which the traditional society rests – confronts new forces of change. In the Hispanic world, the family unit has historically been a microcosm of society as a whole. Within it, the woman was expected to assume a role of docile dependence. But male dominance began to be challenged after the Second World War as women acquired certain legal rights previously denied them, including, in many republics, the right to vote in national elections as well as economic safeguards in marriage and other contractual situations. It may well be, however, that nothing has contributed to the liberation of women so much as the increasing availability of birth control devices, the use of which lies with them. In 1967 Colombia, despite the campaign waged by the powerful Catholic Church against the use of birth control devices, was the world's fourth largest consumer of contraceptive pills per thousand fertile women, behind the United States, Australia and Belgium. This was striking evidence that in one fundamental aspect of family relations the women of Spanish America need no longer accept the dictates of the male, and that they have at hand the means to challenge the whole cultural pattern of *machismo*, which rests essentially on the concept of male supremacy. Can society as a whole continue to be structured along traditional lines once the relationship of dependence and dominance within society's basic unit begins to break down?

Despite its attitude towards birth control, the Catholic Church now seems often to be embarking upon policies that threaten the traditional society. The resurgence of its influence that became discernible in several republics during the 1960s was based in part upon the insistence by an articulate minority of churchmen that the lower classes discard their dependence upon the paternalism of others and acquire genuine power to demand from society what in justice is due to them.

Reform-minded churchmen in Spanish America came increasingly in the 1960s to speak of a process they called *concientización*. By this they meant imparting a sense of awareness and class solidarity to workers, and beyond this an appreciation of the potential power that workers have for shaping their own and their country's destiny. *Concientización* represents a new approach to an old endeavour, sporadically undertaken in Spanish America, to awaken the masses. Liberals and positivists sought to awaken the masses to their potential as capitalists, and thereby to transform society. Arielists sought to awaken the masses to their potential as humanists, and thereby to prevent basic social change. Clergymen now speak of the need to awaken the masses to their capacity to achieve social justice and, in the process, substantially to alter the traditional society.

Spokesmen of *concientización* lay heavy stress on material incentives, conceived of not so much in individual terms as in a collective effort to achieve the common good and a better life style for all society. The fact that the Church, as in the past, claims the right to define the common good, and that it is priests who insist upon directing the awakening of the masses, has led many observers to see *concientización* as a bid by the Church for augmented temporal power within a society facing the likelihood, if not the inevitability, of profound change.

A different dimension is given to *concientización* by the fact that many of its foremost advocates are those Catholic clergymen from the United States who, in notably increasing numbers, have served in Spanish America since the Second World War, helping to offset that area's chronic shortage of priests. These priests are concerned with awakening the masses and seem intent upon introducing into Spanish America the social patterns of their native country. In a way, they are writing a new chapter in the history of United States cultural imperialism.

Changing social and economic attitudes are, of course, widely in evidence among Spanish America's native born churchmen. To a considerable extent these attitudes reflect a changing emphasis in theology. In the past the Church tended to use the paternalistic solicitude and supernatural powers of the priesthood to assure the masses of redemption and to attach very little importance to the natural virtue and initiative of the individual layman. Since the Second World War, however, and especially since the Second Vatican Council (1962–65), a number of Spanish American theologians have placed greater stress on the role of the individual conscience in attaining salvation. With rewards in the next world coming to be equated with the independent exercise of individual initiative, in a way that suggests to some observers an accommodation with the spirit of Protestantism, it will be difficult to persuade men that rewards in this world can best be gained through dependence and passivity.

An additional source of crisis for the traditional society arises from the growing divisions within the ranks of the dominant culture. Expansion of the educational system, and a rate of economic growth that would seem spectacular were its effects not more than offset by the population increase, have contributed to the rapid proliferation of the middle sectors. Their ranks have swelled to such an extent that they can no longer realistically dream of entry into the upper-class world, and consequently many of their representative figures no longer tend to identify automatically with that world and to defend its privileges. Instead, some middle-sector leaders speculate for a variety of reasons upon what could be accomplished by destroying the upper classes and channelling their financial resources into entirely new undertakings.

Undoubtedly many bourgeois elements throughout Spanish America have come to reject the established order because they find their material security threatened by the chronic underdevelopment of their national economies. Despairing of being able to satisfy even minimal material ambitions through hard work and individual initiative, they are ready to repudiate the values of classical liberalism and surrender individual liberties to a state which can, they believe, accomplish economic miracles through the imposition of rigid controls. They expect that such a state will provide them with material security and are ready to a certain degree to accept that this may entail the enforcement of Marxist solutions.

Other members of the Spanish American middle sectors, no longer able realistically to dream of rising into the upper ranks of society, have come to accept their bourgeois existence as permanent. Optimistic about their ability to survive in a competitive and materialistic way of life, and proud of their capitalist skills, they do not aspire to a basically different position. Men of this type are coming to constitute a true middle class – as opposed to the old middle sectors who regarded their status as transient and acted to some degree as the hangers-on and sycophants of the privileged few – and as such they no longer defend automatically the traditional upper classes. They are, in fact, more likely to seek the curtailment or elimination, rather than the preservation, of upper-class privileges and immunities.

Certain Spanish Americans, best described as 'bourgeois Communists', can be categorized for all practical purposes as middle class. Men of this type appear to be pleased by the gradualism of the Moscow-directed variety of Communism, whose spokesmen have insisted since 1935 that Spanish America must undergo a massive capitalist development before the time becomes propitious for the dictatorship of the proletariat. Bourgeois Communists see no inconsistency in professing Communism – a fashionable intellectual and sometimes a politically advantageous position – while at the same time sharpening their capitalist skills and amassing fortunes. Ostensibly they are preparing the way for Communism, but they are confident that it will not arrive in time to interfere with their capitalist pursuits.

It is, of course, hazardous to generalize about the Spanish American middle groups, for, as already noted, they constitute anything but a monolithic force. Even among the largely middle-class – or middle-sector – university students attitudes vary greatly. A recent study of Chilean university students by Frank Bonilla and Myron Glazer, which certainly reflects conditions in other republics as well, shows that students whose inadequate secondary education and low entrance qualifications exclude them from faculties such as engineering and medicine – particularly those in the faculties of philosophy and education whose prospects of lucrative future employment are small – tend to be frustrated and radical, or even revolutionary. On the other hand, engineering students, who have the best expectations of future status and salary, are the most closely tied to the existing order.

At the other extreme, there are still many Spanish Americans who remain convinced that the only way to avoid unprecedented and calamitous upheavals is to repudiate altogether the economic goals that inspire the developed countries of the western world. They include a few intellectuals who see the solution in a conservative Catholicism of a type that was common before the Second Vatican Council. On the lines once proposed by Manuel Gálvez in Argentina, they call for a spiritualization of all sectors of Spanish American society, a spiritualization which they equate with the rekindling of Catholic fervour and which they say must begin at the top. Their hope is that if the upper and middle classes, taking to heart the other-worldly precepts of traditional Hispanic Catholicism, cease to present an example of unbridled acquisitiveness, the masses will in time curb their desire for material advance, thereby eliminating the cause of social revolution. Even in Venezuela, where the materialism of the ruling classes is blatant and undisguised, a few intellectuals, among them Carriacolo Parra Pérez and Mario Briceño-Iragorry, continue to cling to this hope.

With Catholicism's declining influence immediately after the Second World War and the later cleavage between Catholic traditionalists and Catholic innovators, even the most ardent of the faithful began to despair of reversing the tide of secularism, and a new group of anti-clerical humanists gained a wide intellectual following. Many of them unorthodox Marxists, these men preached a radicalized version of the Arielist creed of the turn of the century. Convinced that Spanish America was destined to fall further and further behind the already advanced countries of the western world in the quest for material development, they rejected overriding concern with economic progress as a valid stimulus for any level of society. They advocated instead the search for fulfilment through spiritual development. For these secular humanists the bourgeoisie was not an élite capable of leading Spanish America forward to better things but rather a self-interested class pursuing false ideals that had to be repudiated for the common good.

Some of these developments, together with factors peculiar to the island itself, contributed to the collapse of the old order in Cuba and led to the emergence, for the first time in the history of Spanish America, of a society radically different from the traditional one.

13 Castro's Cuba and the Response to New Challenges

When the tyrant Gerardo Machado fell from power in 1933, Cuba was convulsed by the beginnings of a social revolution. In a situation not unlike that which arose towards the end of the 1950s, Cubans from nearly all walks of life demanded a radical break with the conditions that had made their republic the pawn of unprincipled politicians, often in league with United States interests. During the two turbulent years after Machado's withdrawal it seemed that a cresting revolutionary wave would carry all before it. However, divisions and confusion of purpose among the advocates of change, combined with shrewd leadership on the part of the Cuban defenders of the *status quo* and effective diplomatic action on the part of the United States, brought the revolution to nothing. The result was the emergence of Fulgencio Batista as the principal guardian of the old order in Cuba, although the sergeant who had overnight promoted himself to colonel did not actually occupy the presidential office until 1940.

Combining force with suavity and astuteness and taking full advantage of United States assistance, Batista had snuffed out the revolutionary threat by the end of 1935. For a time, he settled into a period of relatively enlightened rule, introducing certain reforms so as to shore up Cuba's creaking social, economic and political structure. Gradually, however, Batista – a man of lower middle-class origins whose appearance suggested Spanish, Chinese and African extraction (associates of the rapidly rising adventurer generally found it expedient to ignore appearances and to deny the latter two elements) – became a symbol of the corrupt society he served. Its representatives seem to have convinced themselves that, with the revolutionary threat crushed, almost endless time had been purchased for the old way of life and that the day of reckoning could be indefinitely postponed.

Ramón Grau San Martín, who served as president between 1944 and 1948, was an even more egregious symbol of the corruption of Cuban society. Hugh Thomas, whose book *Cuba, The Pursuit of Freedom* (1971) may well be the best single-volume history of a Latin American republic, describes the Grau régime as 'an orgy of theft ill-disguised by emotional nationalistic speeches'. Grau, Thomas adds, 'did more than any other single man to kill the hope of democratic practice in Cuba'. Nor did the situation improve during the ensuing four-year presidential term of Carlos Prío Socarrás. Gangsterism, political assassination and overt corruption continued to be the order of the day.

If corruption was everywhere in evidence in Cuba, so also was United States capital. Continuing to control nearly 40 per cent of sugar production, United States capital moved into less significant but more visible enterprises, such as gambling, prostitution and vice. In the degradation that Cuba underwent in the period between the mid-1930s and the mid-1950s, United States and native capitalists seemed to be inseparable partners.

In many Spanish American republics, especially from the 1920s onwards, the close relationship between United States and native capitalists had operated at least indirectly to the advantage of the lower classes. With the money generated by the operation of foreign enterprise, governments had found the means to finance broad social programmes. In the Cuba of the 1930s, 1940s and 1950s, however, such social benefits were little in evidence. On the contrary, the ruling classes increasingly adopted the prejudices of classical liberalism in their most extreme form, assuming that poverty was the result of vice and of the alleged racial inferiority of the largely Negroid lower classes, and that, far from deserving charity, the latter should be chastened by hard work and exploitation. Responding to these circumstances, the lower classes began to show signs of restlessness. It is not difficult to understand their sense of grievance against the prevailing social and economic structure.

In rural Cuba, the spread of the sugar plantation – over half of the cultivable land was devoted to cane – had created a factory situation. On the sugar *latifundia*, a wage-earning proletariat replaced a landowning peasantry. This proletariat enjoyed neither the security afforded by the traditional paternalism of a manorial economy nor the benefits of the new form of paternalism that most Spanish American governments had begun to extend to urban labourers at a point early in the twentieth century. They were expected to survive in a competitive, capitalist world; yet conditions which they were powerless to alter made it extremely difficult for them to do so.

In the 1950s, the proportion of unemployed workers remained about three times higher than in the United States. Illiteracy, which declined appreciably in the first quarter of the century, levelled off at a fairly constant plateau. Furthermore, in the 1950s the proportion of children of school age attending primary school was lower than in the 1920s. About half the Cuban population went altogether without schooling, and this in a country which enjoyed one of the highest per capita income figures for all Latin America – more than $500 in the late 1950s – and where capital resources were available to provide educational opportunities as well as adequate

54 Rafael Moreno's *The Farm* (1943), an idealized view of life in rural, pre-revolutionary Cuba.

social services for the poor, had there been a will to do so. Fernando Ortiz describes social-economic conditions in these terms:

> A large part of the working class of Cuba has to live all year on wages earned during two or three months, and the whole lower class suffers from this seasonal work system, being reduced to a status of poverty with an inadequate, vitamin-deficient diet consisting principally of rice, beans and tubers, which leaves it undernourished and the ready prey of hookworm, tuberculosis, malaria and other diseases.

It is not surprising that from the moment he first gained public attention, when he stormed the Moncada Barracks in Santiago de Cuba on 26 July 1953, Fidel Castro drew significant support from Cuba's lower classes by his promises of social justice.

In making a revolutionary situation, however, the alienation of Cuba's middle classes probably was more significant than the discontent of the masses. Numerous factors contributed to this alienation, among them disillusion with bourgeois existence. Just how widespread this disillusion was cannot be accurately gauged, but a good deal of the literature produced by Cubans in the period between the fall of Machado and the rise of Castro attests to its existence.

Traditionally, in the Hispanic world, the middle sectors have not accepted business as a permanent way of life, but have regarded it rather as a stage they must pass through on their way into the upper ranks of society where money-making as an end in itself is disdained and gracious living, prodigality and culture are held to be of primary importance. Ever since the seventeenth century in Spanish America, and considerably before that in Castile, successful merchants and businessmen used their accumulated wealth to gain admission into the higher spheres of society and thereby into a more congenial, less obsessively capitalist, way of life.

In Cuba, however, no true aristocracy existed which the bourgeoisie could hope to join so as to liberate itself from the continuing pursuit of money. Although there were more Cuban millionaires per head of population in pre-revolutionary Cuba than in any other country of Latin America, there was no upper class in the old sense of the term. Joint-stock companies, not individuals, owned the sugar *latifundia*, and the richest Cubans were almost all of them businessmen and stockholders in various enterprises. 'Elsewhere in Latin America', Thomas writes, 'rich businessmen became landowners; in Cuba rich landowners became businessmen.' The bourgeois existence of a Cuban middle class, which had usurped for its members the position once occupied by an aristocracy, understandably repelled many idealistic Cubans, who aspired to something higher than an existence dedicated to the endless pursuit of wealth and who possessed a sense of social justice. Furthermore, unlike the situation in Venezuela since 1958, the bourgeois capitalists who ran the state did not rule with sufficient honesty and concern for national interest to gain legitimacy for the government.

Illegally grabbing the presidential office in 1952, during his final seven years of power Batista alienated many bourgeois elements who had no desire for fundamental socio-economic change but who did demand political reform. The fact that businessmen, merchants, bankers and various entrepreneurs – their numerical strength estimated at about 100,000 – extended the most conspicuous and consistent support to Batista brought the business community into serious disrepute. Thus its members were in a weak position to oppose the well organized Communists, who quickly gained control over the army and other groups on which Castro depended after he finally defeated the Batista forces at the end of 1958.

Within the Spanish American context, it is not strange that many of the alienated and disillusioned middle-class intellectuals who sought social and not just political reform turned towards Marxism, or at least to the heterodox strains of Marxist thought which through the years have exercised a vast appeal to Spanish American humanists who reject the profit motive and the capitalist ethic. In Marxism they found a formula for attaining a degree of daily security that permits men to take up the pursuit of a fuller human existence, even if the cost is dependence upon a paternalistic, but authoritarian or even totalitarian, government. Nor is it surprising, finally, that Cubans who rejected liberal values and the capitalist ethic turned not only against a national plutocracy but also against the United States which, rightly or wrongly, has been regarded by Spanish American humanists as the embodiment of a dehumanizing, bourgeois, materialistic approach to life.

Given the strength of anti-capitalist sentiment throughout much of the Hispanic world it was almost certain that sooner or later a leader would arise who would seek the liquidation of capitalism. And, given the alienation of many middle-class Cuban intellectuals produced in part by the way capitalism operated in Cuba during the twenty-five years following Batista's initial rise to power, it is not surprising that this leader appeared in Cuba. No one, however, could have predicted the charismatic power of the leadership provided by the man who is one of the most effective orators ever produced in the American hemisphere.

What makes the Cuban situation without precedent in the history of Spanish America is the success of Fidel Castro in accomplishing, at least in the short run, what José Carlos Mariátegui and like-minded intellectuals thought most likely to be achieved in Peru and elsewhere by means of the Indian example: namely, the restructuring of society so as to reduce all its citizens to dependence upon a totalitarian, but also a compassionate and charitable, state that takes from each according to his abilities and gives to each according to his needs. At least in theory, the distinction between dominant and sub-cultures has been eliminated in Cuba; the goal of Castro's revolutionary party has been to inculcate in all sections of society the non-individualistic, non-capitalist way of life previously confined to the lower classes. In the view of its admirers, whose judgment may be influenced by wishful thinking, Castro's Cuba, alone among the Spanish American republics, has undergone a revolution, the end result of which has been fraternalism – that is, the interdependence of all sections of the population in a one-culture state.

Obviously, if the tiny Cuban élite that manages the revolutionary processes proliferates, and if its members pursue their own economic interests, it may eventually turn into another privileged class. So far, however, the Cuban leaders, who have been influenced by the ideology of Chinese Communism, have attempted to suppress capitalist motives throughout society and to infuse the top leadership groups with disdain for material rewards. Instead, emphasis has been placed on moral inducements, including national pride, and on imparting a new sense of dignity and importance to the previously ignored masses. People are encouraged to find satisfaction in participation in the activities of local and functional groups, while rigidly controlled government propaganda and education are mobilized in the attempt to forge a new Cuba liberated from the passion for individual gain. The Argentine-born revolutionary 'Che' Guevara played a key role in devising this programme and in championing it before an initially dubious Castro – who readily admits the difficulties he had in living down some of his youthful bourgeois leanings. Steps were even taken to eliminate the use of money in a broad variety of transactions.

In 1967 Castro told K. S. Karol, an uprooted Polish Marxist and admirer of Mao Tse-tung:

> The Chinese may be doing interesting experiments but we are trying to go much farther than they have. Money remains the core of their social program, even though its sights are set on equality, while the Russians deliberately encourage differences in income. We intend to get rid of the whole money myth, rather than tamper with it. We want to abolish money altogether.

Castro did not point out, perhaps he was unaware, that the attempt to replace material with moral incentives was a paramount feature of the Soviet experience in the 1920s and 1930s, and that it was ultimately abandoned as a failure.

Cuba's revolutionaries, of course, like reform-minded Churchmen elsewhere in Spanish America intent upon carrying out *concientización*, do lay stress on material incentives; but these are not conceived of in individual terms. Instead, men are exhorted to a collective effort to achieve the common good and a better life style for the various functional units of which they are a part and for society as a whole.

In order to achieve the objectives of the Cuban revolution it was necessary to attempt the collectivization of the entire economy and, in conjunction with this, to expropriate or confiscate all privately owned means of production. Merely to nationalize the largest and most politically vulnerable sectors of the economy, as happened in Mexico and Bolivia, would not have sufficed. In Cuba, the revolution sought to crush private capitalism at every level of society and did not shirk from expelling a considerable proportion of those who clung most tenaciously to a capitalist outlook – by 1970 some 650,000 Cubans had found a refuge in the United States and 95,000 of them had become citizens. The expulsions, combined with voluntary departures, may have resulted initially in a serious economic setback, but they were indispensable if the country were to attain the ideological solidarity required to forge a nation. For similar purposes, and with similar economic consequences, Spain had expelled her Jewish population in 1492.

As a result of his revolution Castro won economic independence from the United States. For this the price he had to pay was economic, and to a

55 In this poster celebrating Cuba's annual Day of the Heroic Guerrilla, the face of 'Che' Guevara dominates the South American continent. Reality was rather different: Cuban attempts to extend their revolution finally foundered in 1967 with 'Che's' death in Bolivia.

lesser extent, political dependence upon the Soviet Union. Psychologically, however, the new dependence has not been unduly oppressive. Cuban leaders can look upon themselves as partners with the leaders of other Communist nations, and even to some extent as rivals, in seeking the best means, in ever-changing world conditions, for applying the prescription 'from each according to his abilities, to each according to his needs'. Moreover, economic dependence on Russia does not prevent Cuba from questioning the Moscow interpretation of Marxism-Leninism, from siding ideologically with China, or from aspiring to play the role of mediator in the ideological clashes between the two major Communist powers.

However minor a power it may be within the Communist world, Cuba cuts a considerably more conspicuous figure there than it did within the capitalist world. This is an intangible reward of its change in international alignment, the importance of which is generally overlooked in the country that dominated Cuba economically before 1959. While it is legitimate to point out the economic failures that have followed in the wake of Cuba's revolution, it must also be remembered that national dignity cannot be measured exclusively in terms of gross national product. Far more than their rivals in the Communist world, United States observers of Cuba suffer from a narrowness of vision that allows them to discern only economic factors in assessing post-revolutionary conditions.

In his 26 July 1970 address Castro made a remarkable assessment of the revolution's accomplishments and failures and also of its ideological framework. The background of this speech must be taken into account.

56 Castro and the Soviet leader Nikita Khrushchev; although their accord appeared to mark the end of the principle of 'America for the Americans', first set down in the Monroe Doctrine, Khrushchev gave way to United States pressure in October 1962 and withdrew the Soviet missiles he had sent to Cuba.

57 Castro lends a hand with the sugar crop.

When they initially came to power, the revolutionaries played down the importance of sugar and sought to achieve industrialization and economic diversification. Their programmes resulted in serious economic deterioration and threatened the ability of the government to supply the social services that had been a key feature of the revolution. By 1964, therefore, the island had reverted to reliance on a sugar economy. Five years later, Castro staked his régime's prestige on the pledge that Cuba would produce an unheard-of crop of 10 million tons of sugar in 1970 – an amount which, if achieved, would still have meant that the island was producing less sugar per head of population than in 1925. As it turned out, the crop came to 8·5 million tons (an all-time record in absolute terms), and Castro sought to explain this failure, as well as many others, to approximately half a million Cubans gathered in Havana's Revolutionary Square to hear his address.

Castro began by stressing that Cuba's population during the time he had been in power had increased from 6,547,000 to 8,256,464. He pointed out in addition that a high percentage of the population was either under the age of seventeen or else over the working age, circumstances which placed a tremendous strain upon the country's economic resources. He claimed that spending on social security, public health and education had increased from 213·8 million pesos (pesos are generally valued on a par with the dollar) in 1958 to 850 million in 1970, noting that in this last year an additional 350 million pesos were allotted to 'defence'. During this same period school enrolment had risen from 936,723 to 2,289,464 – not counting children in day-care centres. Castro then proceeded to describe in minute detail the virtual collapse of most sectors of the Cuban economy, attributing the situation partly to his own ignorance and that of other revolutionary leaders. 'I believe', he stated, 'that we, the leaders of this Revolution, have cost the people too much in our process of learning.'

Continuing his speech, Castro observed:

Today the citizen feels that the state should solve his problems. And he is right. This is really a collective mentality, a socialist mentality. Today everything is expected from the administrative apparatus and especially from the political apparatus that represents it. Today it is not possible to depend on individual efforts and means, as it was in the past.

Castro then came to a central feature of his address as he dwelt on the need for Cuba to produce more so that the state could supply the legitimate economic needs of the island's population. In line with this he stressed the necessity for every worker to assume greater responsibility to maximize productivity, noting that this could not be achieved through brawn but only through brains. So as to enlist workers in the quest of greater collective productivity, Castro recommended establishing a collective body for managing each plant. 'Why shouldn't we', he asked, 'begin to introduce representatives of the factory's workers into its management? Why not have confidence? Why not put our trust in that tremendous proletarian spirit of the men who, at times in torn shoes and clothes, nevertheless keep up production?'

Candid as this speech appeared to be, Castro in some ways avoided confessing the truly enormous dimensions of the Cuban economic failure. He did not point out that the island's food production had declined in per capita, and possibly even in absolute, terms since 1958 – in spite of the fact that in the 1960s Cuba received more economic aid per capita than any nation in the world and that most of the funds involved in the remarkably high annual investment rate of nearly 30 per cent of the gross national product had been earmarked for agriculture. Nor, in the light of subsequent developments, did Castro appear to be altogether ingenuous in the remedies he recommended. He did not initiate factory worker groups so as to allow labourers to participate directly in decisions about production. Instead he resorted to more, not less, centralization and also to more militarization as he stepped up the penetration of the 'Rebel Army' into key positions of economic and political control.

Castro also responded to the economic crisis by swinging back towards acceptance of the money economy and reliance on material incentives. In 1972 he devised a programme to reward the island's most productive workers with priority for the purchase of television sets, radios, refrigerators and other scarce consumer goods. Thus Castro demonstrated once more that he is as much the pragmatic humanist as the ideologist. In fact, except for Castro's more repressive measures, there exist striking similarities between Castro and Miguel Primo de Rivera, Spain's bumbling but affable and well-intentioned dictator of the 1920s. The lack of ideological consistency was among the many factors Norman Gall had in mind when he wrote in 1971: 'Indeed, with each passing year Cuba appears less a socialist republic than a classic Latin American military dictatorship with Marxist-Leninist trappings.'

In the first dozen years of his rule Castro proved singularly unsuccessful in exporting his revolution. Initially, before internal failures became a factor, the basic reason for this was undoubtedly because the Cuban revolution departed so totally from the Hispanic tradition of a two-culture society. In addition, circumstances in many Spanish American republics were unfavourable. The areas closest at hand during the early years of the Cuban revolution were the least inclined to alter the established order. Mexico had already had a social revolution, and though by this time many features of Mexican society badly needed overhauling, its total collapse did not seem imminent. Venezuela had benefited more than most parts of Spanish America from a process of evolution. The large and well established capitalist bourgeoisie was relatively secure, satisfied with the country's political leadership, and a Cuban-style revolution seemed unnecessary. In Colombia the situation was different. Many Colombians may have felt the need for revolution, even if not necessarily of the Cuban type; but they were demoralized by the lingering consequences of the earlier abortive revolution, *la violencia*, and were psychologically unprepared to attempt a fresh confrontation with the old order.

Further afield, it soon became clear that Bolivia did not provide a fertile field for planting a 'liberation movement' patterned on the Cuban model. The movement led by 'Che' Guevara in 1967 suffered from the fact that the Bolivian Left, although dissatisfied with the prevailing order, was as much nationalistic as revolutionary. It resented the attempt of a foreigner to assume the leadership, all the more so because he was an Argentinian, and as such stigmatized by the long-standing antipathy of Bolivian politicians and intellectuals towards the citizens of a country regarded as an imperialistic menace to national interests. On the other hand, it was not easy for Guevara to interest the peasants in his cause, seeing he could not even speak their Indian dialect.

Nor would it seem that Uruguayans are more inclined than Bolivians or the haughty, nationalistic Argentinians to follow the example of Cuba. Uruguay may well be moving towards a revolutionary situation, but Uruguayans and Argentinians, priding themselves on the whiteness of their populations and upon their moderation, have traditionally been critical of the volatility and emotionalism of Cubans, which they attribute to the high percentage of Negroid blood in the population, as well as to the climate. Similar attitudes prevail among Chileans, and the lengthy visit of Fidel Castro to Chile in 1971 may well have done more to impede than to facilitate President Allende's attempts to lead the country into socialism.

Even the renowned Liberator Simón Bolívar failed to bring about Spanish American unity, his hopes dashed by the rivalries, jealousies and national prejudices that appeared before independence had so much as been achieved. Castro, who sometimes likes to pose as the man upon whom Bolívar's mantle has fallen, and who frequently resorts to one of the Liberator's favourite histrionic devices of offering to resign before large and friendly audiences, seems unlikely to achieve greater success than his heroic predecessor in the quest for supra-national goals, institutions and models for Spanish America.

When a revolutionary situation developed in Peru in the 1960s, its leaders appeared to wish Castro well in his domestic reforms but remained adamantly opposed to following the Cuban example in their own land. In fact, their underlying intention may well have been to prevent changes of the type and magnitude produced by the Cuban revolution. Nevertheless, the revolution led by the Peruvian military has resulted in innovations of great significance, and for this reason requires separate consideration.

14 The Peruvian Military and the Response to New Challenges

At mid-twentieth century, Peru remained divided between a fairly progressive, modernized coastal area and a highland or *sierra* region still largely inhabited by unassimilated Indians, where a backward, semifeudal economy prevailed. Much of the *sierra's* expanse lay in the hands of some 33,000 private landowners. Of these, 1233 held property of more than 2500 acres each and controlled nearly 80 per cent of the land under cultivation or used for pasture. On many of the large estates labourers, known as *yanaconas*, were virtual serfs who were given the right to use tiny plots of land, often no more than a furrow or two, in exchange for contributing a specified number of days of labour throughout the year to the estate owner. The most immediate problem, however, centred on the approximately 5000 Indian *comunidades* of highland Peru which had managed through the centuries to cling to at least a small portion of collective property. While the great landowners continued their efforts to expropriate these lands, an expanding Indian population placed new demands upon the limited resources of the *comunidades*.

In the 1950s and 1960s this situation gave rise to a renewal of sporadic violence in the *sierra*, which a handful of Marxist militants hoped to use to fan a revolution that would fulfil some of the ideals of González Prada and Mariátegui. But very little came of their efforts, because of their own ineptness as well as the effects of reforms initiated by the government in Lima.

In 1962 President Manuel Prado y Ugarteche was overthrown, just before the completion of his second term of office; after a year of military rule, the 1963 election brought to the presidency an engaging man who seemed to be the saviour of traditional Peru. Fernando Belaúnde Terry, a member of an aristocratic family notable for its intellectuals and politicians, enjoyed good connections with the Church and the military and at the same time had a flare for the dramatic and a knack of exciting the masses. The dynamic president, an architect trained at the University of Texas, announced a programme aimed simultaneously at encouraging the capitalism of coastal Peru and the socialism said still to be characteristic of *sierra*, Indian Peru. The response at first was enthusiastic. The bulk of the electorate was ready to co-operate in seeking national harmony and to abandon both the old crusade to force the coastal way of life on the Indian and the belligerent drive from the other side to impose the Indian way of life, real and imagined, on the coastal dweller.

As a first step towards realization of his policies, Belaúnde gained congressional approval of land reform legislation designed to take some property from the owners of the huge estates in the *sierra* for redistribution among the Indian *comunidades*. At the same time Indians were encouraged to become active participants in co-operative associations intended to increase efficiency in the utilization of land owned collectively by the *comunidades* and to provide a basis for local self-government. If successfully carried out, Belaúnde's programme would have ensured the Indians an existence relatively free from individualist and capitalist intrusion and at the same time given them a greater sense of participation by allowing them a voice in semi-autonomous associations.

The president's policies, unfortunately, were never resolutely pursued, in no small part because of congressional opposition spearheaded by *Apristas*, which found expression outside the parliamentary chambers in the irresponsible journalism of Pedro Beltrán's daily newspaper *La Prensa*. Belaúnde's policies did, however, help to put an end to Indian violence.

58 Lima slum-dwellers occupy state land in the Pamplona district of the capital city: since the 1950s especially, the squalid living conditions endured by the rapidly growing urban lower classes have constituted one of the major problems confronting Peru – and every other Spanish American republic as well.

Yet virtually no progress was made towards realizing the long-term goals. The architect-president planned, by means of vast road and colonization projects, to drain off the surplus population of the *sierra* to unutilized lands in the east. But, largely because of lack of funds, the project proved abortive, and the influx into the coastal cities of the west, where economic resources were already inadequate to cope with mounting population pressures, continued unabated. Essentially, it was the problems of coastal Peru, where Belaúnde hoped to stimulate greater capitalist efficiency, that led to the fall of the visionary president.

By the early 1960s the middle classes, accounting probably for about 20 per cent of the country's population, had come to hold the balance of political power. A steady demographic shift had contributed to this development. In the years between 1940 and 1961, more than 15 per cent of the rural population moved to the cities. Many of the new arrivals swelled the ranks of the urban proletariat. Some, however, succeeded within a fairly short period in entering the lower ranks at least of the middle classes. The rapid expansion of industry facilitated their entry. By 1963 industry produced 19·5 per cent of the gross national product, almost matching agriculture which accounted for 19·9 per cent. A further factor facilitating the growth of middle sectors was the rapid expansion of higher educational facilities. University education in Peru had long ago ceased to be the exclusive privilege of the aristocracy, and by 1964 some 48,000 students were attending the thirty institutions that claimed university status – an increase from 3839 students at seven universities in 1940.

At the same time, however, there was mounting evidence that Peru's emergent middle class would have to wage a concerted struggle to maintain for their children the economic and social level they had attained for themselves. Economic opportunities were not keeping pace with the increase in population. Between 1940 and 1961 the Peruvian population rose from 7 million to over 11 million, but possibilities of employment in industry, mining, commerce and the service industries did not keep pace. In 1963, the Peruvian economy was providing only some 10,000 new jobs each year, while most economists agreed that within ten years, if the country hoped to avoid staggering unemployment levels and economic stagnation, the annual number of new openings would have to rise to at least 100,000. Moreover, notwithstanding the remarkable expansion of higher education facilities, Peru's universities in 1964 admitted only 13·6 per cent of applicants, partly through lack of space and partly because many candidates were inadequately prepared. At the same time Peru was suffering from an inflation which, although mild in comparison with most other Spanish American countries, still placed a strain on all save the wealthiest classes.

The result was that many middle-class Peruvians felt desperately insecure, and Belaúnde could accomplish little during the years he was in office (1963–68) towards easing their mounting sense of insecurity. Although his stated purpose was to stimulate capitalist enterprise in the coastal areas, economic development did not progress sufficiently either to provide adequate opportunities for the middle classes or to generate the resources necessary to finance the programmes of social assistance on which the urban lower classes were dependent.

In many respects Peru's officer corps constituted a microcosm of the country's hard-pressed middle sectors. By the 1960s most of the officers, even generals, came from a middle-class background, and felt a sense of exclusion and frustration in their relations with the top social élite, which they began to refer to with increasing disdain as a plutocracy. They did not come from it and could not expect to rise into it even through the most successful military career, and as conditions deteriorated they were increasingly willing either to eliminate it altogether or else to force various reforms upon its members, through which they would be disciplined into using their capital in a manner more consonant with the national interest.

But even though their attitude towards the élite hardened, nevertheless the Peruvian military retained to a large extent the traditional bourgeois outlook towards the lower classes. They could not bring themselves to identify with the proletariat; and they feared displacement by mass movements that might turn to the Cuban revolution for ideological inspiration. They were willing to deal paternalistically both with the Indians and with the urban poor, convinced that paternalism was the best means of preventing the uprising of the masses and keeping them in subjection. This very conviction intensified their alienation from the plutocrats who seemed little disposed to carry out the social and economic policies which the officer corps regarded as essential to maintain the *status quo*.

Because they regarded Belaúnde, for all his good intentions, as the prisoner of a plutocracy incapable of reforming a malfunctioning system, and also because they feared an *Aprista* victory in the next presidential election, the military overthrew the chief executive in October 1968 and assumed the direct exercise of political power. They established a dictatorship headed by General Juan Valasco Alvarado, who made up for what he lacked in magnetism and glamour with an aura of hard-working dedication, and announced a far-reaching revolutionary programme with pronounced anti-capitalist overtones. It would, however, be a serious misreading of their intentions to identify this anti-capitalism with Marxism, as many hostile critics in the United States have done. As in other parts of the Hispanic world, criticism of capitalism in Peru is often traditional, non-revolutionary and, at its core, non-Marxist. Indeed, there is much evidence that the anti-capitalism of the Peruvian military government was inspired to a large extent by the idea of avoiding revolutionary change by curbing the excesses of liberal capitalism so as to prevent the disintegration of the two-culture society.

In implementing a bold new programme of agrarian reform, the Peruvian military seized many of the large, privately owned (both by foreigners and natives) sugar and cotton plantations along the coast that had not been affected by the legislation of the Belaúnde administration. These estates were then turned over, always under careful government surveillance, to the partial control of newly organized workers' co-operatives, thereby dealing what it was hoped would be a death-blow against the *Aprista*-led labour unions that in the past had represented coastal agricultural workers. Some observers have seen in the creation of collectivist co-operatives a truly revolutionary measure, but it probably represents nothing more than the old expedient of preventing a challenge to the existing order from below by giving the lower classes the sense of dignity that comes from participating in decisions of most immediate importance to them. To this extent the objective of the military dictatorship seems to be to foster in the coastal proletariat the same collectivist, non-individualistic, non-materialistic values that Belaúnde had sought to fortify among the Indian *comunidades* of the *sierra*.

The anti-capitalism of the Peruvian military régime is directed towards the sub-culture, not towards the dominant culture. It is true that the self-interested plutocracy was attacked for its refusal to accept its social obligations, and the confiscation of the estates of wealthy landowners in the coastal region was an essential move in introducing corporative features into the social and political organization. Nevertheless, the officers do not seem to have envisaged the total destruction of the agrarian capitalists; rather, their object appears to have been to take away their lands and then force them to invest the bonds issued in compensation, and their other capital, in urban, industrial enterprises. As in Mexico under Cárdenas, the objective of the Peruvian military was evidently not to wipe out private capitalism, but rather to discipline private capitalists and persuade them to invest in sectors of the economy they had customarily neglected.

Within Peru, the Catholic Church has enthusiastically backed the revolution. This is scarcely surprising. As elsewhere in Spanish America, both the Church and the military continue to seek to protect their corporate interests and also to maintain the sort of conditions in society that will facilitate the accomplishment of their respective missions. If they can best accomplish these goals by dramatically dissociating themselves from an established ruling class that appears to be doomed, they will not hesitate to take such action.

59 Church and State in unity: a Church dignitary watches a parade by troops of the Peruvian military régime.

Outside Peru, the revolution has been denounced both by Marxists and by United States capitalists; and this is no more surprising than the backing it has received from the Peruvian Church. A system that is anti-capitalist only in relation to the lower classes, but pro-capitalist so far as the middle and upper classes are concerned, is unlikely to commend itself to Marxists, while the champions of the United States way of life could scarcely enthuse over a system that denies the alleged blessings of self-reliance and individual economic initiative to the lower classes.

There are, of course, other and more direct reasons for the hostility of United States capitalist interests towards Peru's military government. The owners of California fishing industries were outraged by Peruvian claims that national sovereignty extended 200 miles into the ocean. Furthermore, it was the policy of the leaders of the revolution to make the country less dependent upon foreign capital, partly because the United States no longer seemed a reliable source of aid and investment. By embarking upon a policy of economic nationalism, the military undoubtedly hoped to enhance its popularity among the masses so as to make its demands for greater efficiency and sacrifice acceptable, and also to acquire better leverage in its attempt to discipline the moneyed classes into becoming more effective and independent capitalists. Symbolism has seemed as important as substance to the Peruvian military in pursuing these goals. The symbolic declaration of economic independence was the expropriation, immediately after the officers took over, of the International Petroleum Company. Once the politically expedient act of expropriating IPC – long the favourite target of economic nationalists – had been made, the military showed their true instincts by quietly encouraging other United States companies to begin exploration for new petroleum reserves.

The Peruvian military revolution may be distasteful to many foreign observers. But what matters is whether it will satisfy Peruvians as a solution which will enable them both to advance towards development and to safeguard a way of life to some extent in harmony with the standards, values and attitudes associated for centuries with the Spanish-speaking countries of the Old and New Worlds. In so far as it operates within the traditional framework of Hispanic life, it is possible that the Peruvian revolution may exercise greater influence within the Hispano-American world than the Cuban attempt to eradicate forever all connection with the old two-culture society.

At its best moments in the past, the Hispanic, corporativist, essentially two-culture society has shown that it is possible for people at all levels of society to find dignity and human realization within a structure that is rooted neither in Marxism nor in liberal democracy. Even if the military revolution should founder, as all movements after all do, because of its leaders' weaknesses and the enormity of the problems confronting them, events in Peru since 1968 may conceivably indicate that the Spanish-speaking peoples of South America have begun to come to grips with the demands of the modern world by seeking to be themselves. No doubt, each of the different nations will do so within the context of its own distinctive traditions, and, if they are to succeed, Peruvians will have to do better than the Argentinians under Perón in finding the proper balance between materialism and spirituality, and between individualism and collectivism.

15 Conclusion

Within Spanish America's dominant culture there were, as the twentieth century began, many different status levels. At the top were the true aristocrats, those best able to lay claim to independence and self-reliance, those least burdened by obligations other than self-imposed ones. In some ways, of course, the aristocracy's independence was illusory. After all, its members were in the final analysis dependent upon the economic goods resulting in part from the labour of the sub-culture. In a world, though, in which economic considerations were supposed to be relegated to the lowest position in a hierarchical structure of values that accorded highest status to what was spiritual, some semblance of economic dependence was not considered galling or demeaning. In fact, the state of semi-economic parasitism in which the true aristocrats lived – in their relationship both to a domestic labour force and to foreign capitalists – was a badge of distinction; for such parasitism attested to their qualifications to engage in activities loftier than the generation of material wealth.

Within the dominant culture, but beneath the aristocracy, was a large group of middle sectors, some of whose members found a place in the professions, services and bureaucracy. Others, lower down the scale, dedicated themselves to economic enterprise, to money-grubbing activities. Members of this last group were necessary to keep the two-culture society economically viable by means of their participation in primary economic production and their preoccupation with the creation of new wealth. They also infused new capital into the aristocracy from time to time, through partnerships of one type or another and often through marriage. Thereby they periodically rescued the aristocracy from the material plight to which it was often reduced by a characteristic disdain for sound economic principles. Thus a tradition, which can be traced back at least to sixteenth-century Castile, was maintained within the Hispanic world.

Although they were necessary, the economically enterprising men of the middle sectors who constituted a bourgeoisie were also to some extent pariahs. At best they were tolerated within a society whose preservation depended upon safeguarding both the sub-culture and the aristocracy from infection by bourgeois values. So long, however, as bourgeois elements regarded their own role with distaste, they posed no challenge to the traditional society. And, to a considerable degree during a good part of the first century following independence in most Spanish American countries, bourgeois groups as often as not maintained an apologetic air about their economic enterprise and sought to win neither the sub-culture nor the aristocracy to their way of life.

This situation changed in various republics around the turn of the century as positivism, evolving out of liberalism, became a powerful ideological and political force. What the spread of at least one type of positivism basically signified was that certain members of the bourgeoisie were ceasing to be apologetic. They were becoming assertive and demanded that the rest of society begin to live in accordance with bourgeois values. Out of new bourgeois assertiveness came increased friction between the dominant and sub-cultures, friction that began to weaken the fabric of the traditional society.

As the threat of social revolution became more evident, an incipient bourgeoisie curtailed its aggressive attempt to transform society, abandoning at least partially the dream of dramatic economic development based upon the awakening and integration of the masses. They settled instead for an economic policy of muddling through by means of reliance on foreign capital. At the same time they reverted, by and large, to their role as defenders of an aristocracy. The dominant culture closed ranks in defence of a society attuned more to aristocratic than to bourgeois values.

By mid-twentieth century, new rifts within the ranks of the dominant culture had produced a dramatically different situation. For a number of reasons the middle sectors were abandoning their concern with preserving the world of traditional aristocratic privileges which, in part because of a startling growth in numbers, they could no longer hope to join. Moreover, in the light of increasing national economic demands, occasioned to a large extent by the population explosion and also by the relative scarcity of foreign capital, it had become clear that society could no longer afford to indulge the non-productive members of a leisure class.

In contrast to what occurred at the time of its abortive bid for power at the turn of the century, an aggressive bourgeoisie may well come to prevail in Spanish America – outside Cuba – in the second half of the twentieth century and eliminate the traditional élite from its important position within the power structure. In such a case, a whole new morality of wealth would be likely to arise, with money-making skills, intended to serve not only individual interests but hopefully the common good as well, coming to be equated with virtue and even with redeeming grace. The technocrats of the lay religious order Opus Dei, who since the late 1950s have set many of Spain's social, economic and political policies, have helped to establish just such a new morality in the Hispanic world. By the early 1970s its expansion into various parts of Spanish America was apparent.

In this respect the bourgeois way is triumphing over the aristocratic way of life within the dominant culture. In another respect, however, the opposite is true; for Spanish America's new middle class seems to be embracing the traditional aristocratic attitudes towards the masses. Racial prejudices, undiminished through the years except in Venezuela, help to account for this. Emerging middle-class leaders in Spanish America do not wish to permit self-assertiveness in men about whose potential they are dubious. Unlike many representative figures of the bourgeoisie in about 1900, who thought it safe to experiment with transforming the masses into self-reliant, individualistic capitalists, many of the recently risen middle-class leaders in contemporary Spanish America accept the characteristic aristocratic viewpoint that nothing should be done which might cause the masses to emerge from their dependence. This will contribute towards the preservation of a largely traditional two-culture society. Despite the many new forces that have begun to work against it since the Second World War, the early extinction of that society is by no means certain.

Preservation of some features of the traditional society in Spanish America is not necessarily to be deplored. If various projections for the future made by knowledgeable men are correct, if the rich nations are destined to become proportionately richer and the poor proportionately poorer, then perhaps it will be kinder to the men of the sub-culture not to awaken their expectations of greater material wealth or to encourage their desire for a system that will give to them substantially beyond their needs. If in the years ahead the Spanish American masses can find compensation in non-material rewards for an existence of material privation, then it will be a presumptuous man indeed who contends that the traditional estate in which they live is one of underdevelopment.

GENERAL ANALYSIS

Anderson, C. W. *Politics and Economic Change in Latin America: The Governing of Restless Nations*. Princeton 1967.

Blakemore, H. and Smith, C. T. (eds.) *Latin America: Geographical Perspectives*. New York /London 1972.

Chilcote, R. H. *Revolution and Structural Change in Latin America: A Bibliography on Ideology, Development, and the Radical Left, 1930–1965*, 2 vols. Stanford 1969.

Dealy, G. 'Prolegomena on the Spanish American Political Tradition' in *The Hispanic American Historical Review*, XLVIII (1968), 37–58.

Gott, R. *Guerrilla Movements in Latin America*. Garden City 1972.

Heath, D. B. and Adams, R. N. (eds.) *Contemporary Cultures and Societies of Latin America: A Reader in the Social Anthropology of Middle and South America and the Caribbean*. New York 1965.

Horowitz, I. L. (ed.) *Masses in Latin America*. New York 1970.

Humphreys, R. A. *Tradition and Revolt in Latin America*. London 1969.

Lambert, J. *Latin America: Social Structures & Political Institutions*. Trans. by H. Katel. Berkeley/Los Angeles 1969.

Landsberger, H. A. (ed.) *Latin American Peasant Movements*. Ithaca 1969.

Lipset, S. M. and Solari, A. (eds.) *Elites in Latin America*. New York 1967.

Mander, J. *The Unrevolutionary Society: The Power of Latin American Conservatism in a Changing World*. New York 1969.

Silvert, K. H. *The Conflict Society: Reaction and Revolution in Latin America*. New York 1966 (2nd rev. edn).

Stein, S. J. and Stein, B. H. *The Colonial Heritage of Latin America*. New York 1970.

Tannenbaum, F. *Ten Keys to Latin America*. New York 1962.

Vega, L. M. *Roads to Power in Latin America*. Trans. by R. Rowland. New York 1969.

Wagley, C. *The Latin American Tradition: Essays on the Unity and Diversity of Latin American Culture*. New York 1968.

NATIONALISM, MILITARISM, AND CATHOLICISM

Baily, S. L. (ed.) *Nationalism in Latin America*. New York 1971.

Drekonja, G. 'Religion and Social Change in Latin America' in *Latin American Research Review*, VI (1971), 53–72.

Einaudi, L. R. and Stepan, A. C. *Latin American Institutional Development: Changing Military Perspectives in Peru and Brazil*. Santa Monica 1971.

McAlister, L. N. 'Recent Research and Writings on the Role of the Military in Latin America' in *Latin American Research Review*, II (1966), 5–36.

Mecham, J. L. *Church and State in Latin America*. Chapel Hill 1966 (2nd rev. edn).

Mutchler, D. *The Church as a Political Factor in Latin America: With Particular Reference to Colombia and Chile*. New York 1971.

Smith, D. E. *Religion and Political Development*. Boston 1970.

Turner, F. C. *Catholicism and Political Development in Latin America*. Chapel Hill 1971.

Whitaker, A. P. and Jordan, D. *Nationalism in Contemporary Latin America*. New York 1966.

LABOUR AND THE UNIVERSITY

Alba, V. *Politics and the Labor Movement in Latin America*. Trans. by C. Miller de Zapata. Stanford 1968.

Alexander, R. J. *Organized Labor in Latin America*. New York 1965.

Petersen, J. H. 'Recent Research on Latin American University Students' in *Latin American Research Review*, V (1970), 37–58.

SOCIAL FACTORS

Adams, R. N. et. al. *Social Change in Latin America Today*. New York 1960.

Cárdenas, L. (ed.) *Urbanization in Latin America*. Austin 1967.

Iutaka, S. 'Social Stratification Research in Latin America' in *Latin American Research Review*, I (1965), 7–34.

Johnson, J. J. *Political Change in Latin America: The Emergence of the Middle Sectors*. Stanford 1965 (2nd edn).

Mörner, M. (ed.) *Race and Class in Latin America.* New York 1970.

Schaedel, R. P. (ed.) *Social Change in Latin America.* Atlanta 1968.

FOREIGN INVESTMENT AND ECONOMIC FACTORS

Bernstein, M. (ed.) *Foreign Investment in Latin America.* New York 1965.

Fann, K. T. and Hodges, D. C. (eds.) *Readings in U.S. Imperialism.* Boston 1971.

Furtado, C. *Economic Development of Latin America: A Survey from Colonial Times to the Cuban Revolution.* Trans. by S. Macedo. Cambridge, Eng. 1970.

Glade, W. P. *The Latin American Economies: A Study of Their Institutional Evolution.* New York 1969.

Gordon, W. C. *The Political Economy of Latin America.* New York 1965.

Griffin, K. *Underdevelopment in Spanish America: An Interpretation.* Cambridge, Mass. 1970.

McGreevey, W. P. and Tyrer, R. B. 'Recent Research on the Economic History of Latin America' in *Latin American Research Review,* III (1968), 89–117.

Nisbet, C. T. (ed.) *Latin America: Problems in Economic Development.* New York 1969.

POPULATION PROBLEM

Chaplin, D. (ed.) *Population Policy and Growth in Latin America.* Lexington 1971.

Stycos, J. M. and Arias, J. (eds.) *Population Dilemma in Latin America.* New York 1966.

IDEOLOGY AND INTELLECTUAL HISTORY

Davis, H. E. 'The History of Ideas in Latin America' in *Latin American Research Review,* III (1968), 23–44.

Jorrín, M. and Martz, J. D. (eds.) *Latin American Political Thought and Ideology.* Chapel Hill 1970.

Mijares, A. *Hombres e ideas en América.* Caracas 1940.

Pike, F. B. *Hispanismo, 1898–1936: Spanish Conservatives and Liberals and Their Relations with Spanish America.* Notre Dame 1971.

Stabb, M. S. *In Quest of Identity: Patterns in the Spanish American Essay of Ideas, 1890–1960.* Chapel Hill 1967.

Woodward, R. L. (ed.) *Positivism in Latin America, 1850–1900: Are Order and Progress Reconcilable?* Boston 1971.

MEXICO

Cline, H. F. *Mexico: Revolution to Evolution, 1940–1960.* London 1962.

Cockcroft, J. D. *Intellectual Precursors of the Mexican Revolution.* Austin 1968.

Cosío Villegas, D. (dir.-ed.) *Historia moderna de México.* México 1955–.

González Casanova, P. *Democracy in Mexico.* Trans. by D. Salti. New York 1970.

Hale, C. 'The History of Ideas: Substantive and Methodological Aspects of the Thought of Leopoldo Zea' in *Journal of Latin American Studies,* III (1971), 59–70.

Hansen, R. D. *The Politics of Mexican Development.* Baltimore 1971.

Kahl, J. A. *The Measurement of Modernism: A Study of Values in Brazil and Mexico.* Austin 1968.

Paz, O. *The Labyrinth of Solitude: Life and Thought in Mexico.* Trans. by L. Kemp. New York 1961.

Potash, R. A. 'The Historiography of Mexico Since 1821' in *The Hispanic American Historical Review,* XL (1960), 383–424.

Quirk, R. E. *Mexico.* Englewood Cliffs 1971.

Ramos, S. *Profile of Man and Culture in Mexico.* Trans. by P. G. Earle. Austin 1962.

Romanell, P. *Making of the Mexican Mind.* Notre Dame 1965 (2nd edn).

Ross, S. R. (ed.) *Is the Mexican Revolution Dead?* New York 1966.

Scott, R. E. *Mexican Revolt in Transition.* Urbana 1964 (2nd rev. edn).

Smith, R. F. *The United States and Revolutionary Nationalism in Mexico, 1916–1932.* Chicago/London 1972.

Turner, F. C. *The Dynamic of Mexican Nationalism.* Chapel Hill 1968.

Villoro, L. *Los grandes momentos del indigenismo en México.* México 1950.

Wilkie, J. W. *The Mexican Revolution: Federal Expenditure and Social Change Since 1910.* Berkeley/Los Angeles 1970 (2nd rev. edn).

BOLIVIA

Anstee, M. J. *Bolivia: Gate of the Sun.* New York 1970.

Arnade, C. W. 'The Historiography of Colonial and Modern Bolivia' in *The Hispanic American Historical Review,* XLII (1962), 333–84.

Fifer, J. V. *Bolivia: Land, Location, and Politics Since 1825.* Cambridge, Eng. 1971.

Finot, E. *Nueva historia de Bolivia: ensayo de interpretación sociológica.* La Paz 1954 (2nd edn).

Frankovich, G. *El pensamiento boliviano en el siglo XX.* México 1956.

Heath, D. B. et. al. *Land Reform and Social Revolution in Bolivia.* New York 1969.

Klein, H. S. *Parties and Political Change in Bolivia, 1880–1952.* Cambridge, Eng. 1969.

Lora, G. *Historia del movimiento obrero boliviano,* 2 vols. La Paz 1967–69.

Malloy, J. M. *Bolivia: The Uncompleted Revolution.* Pittsburgh 1970.

Montenegro, C. *Nacionalismo y coloniaje: su expresión histórica en la prensa de Bolivia.* La Paz 1943.

Osborne, H. *Bolivia: A Land Divided.* London/New York 1964 (3rd edn).

VENEZUELA

Arcila Farías, E. et. al. Venezuela independiente, 1810–1960. Caracas 1962.

Bernstein, H. Venezuela & Colombia. Englewood Cliffs 1964.

Betancourt, R. Venezuela: política y petroleo. México 1956.

Brito, F. Venezuela, siglo XX. Habana 1967.

Carrera Damas, G. Historia de la historiografía venezolana. Caracas 1961.

Crist, R. E. and Leahy, E. P. Venezuela: Search for a Middle Ground. New York 1969.

Gilmore, R. L. Caudillism and Militarism in Venezuela, 1810–1910. Athens, Ohio 1964.

Martz, J. D. Acción Democrática: Evolution of a Modern Political Party in Venezuela. Princeton 1966.

Moron, G. A History of Venezuela. Trans. by J. Street. New York 1963.

Nava, J. 'The Illustrious American: The Development of Nationalism in Venezuela Under Antonio Guzmán Blanco' in The Hispanic American Historical Review, XLV (1965), 527–43.

Powell, J. D. Political Mobilization of the Venezuelan Peasant. Cambridge, Mass. 1971.

Rangel, D. A. Capital y desarrollo: la Venezuela agraria. Vol. I, La etapa agraria. Caracas 1969.

Silva Michelena, J. A. The Illusion of Democracy in Dependent Nations. Vol. II in the series The Politics of Change in Venezuela. Cambridge, Mass. 1971.

URUGUAY

Ardao, A. Espiritualismo y positivismo en el Uruguay. Montevideo 1968 (2nd edn).

Graceras, U. Los intelectuales y la política en el Uruguay. Montevideo c. 1968.

Lindahl, G. G. Uruguay's New Path: A Study in Politics During the First Colegiado, 1919–1933. Stockholm 1962.

Oddone, J. A. La formación del Uruguay moderno: la inmigración y el desarrollo económico-social. Buenos Aires 1966.

Pivel Devoto, J. E. Historia de la República Oriental del Uruguay, 1830–1930. Montevideo 1945.

Rama, C. M. Ensayo de sociología uruguaya. Montevideo 1957.

Solari, A. Sociología rural nacional. Montevideo 1958.

Taylor, P. B. Government and Politics in Uruguay. New Orleans 1960.

Vanger, M. I. José Batlle y Ordóñez: The Creator of His Times, 1902–1907. Cambridge, Mass. 1963.

Zum Felde, A. Proceso intelectual del Uruguay. Montevideo 1941.

CHILE

Bauer, A. J. 'Chilean Rural Labor in the Nineteenth Century' in The American Historical Review, 76 (1971), 1059–83.

Burnett, B. G. Political Groups in Chile: The Dialogue Between Order and Change. Austin 1971.

Debray, R. The Chilean Revolution: Conversations with Allende. New York 1972.

Donoso, R. Desarrollo político y social de Chile desde la Constitución de 1833. Santiago de Chile 1942.

Eyzaguirre, J. Fisonomía histórica de Chile. Santiago de Chile 1948.

Frank, A. G. Capitalism and Underdevelopment in Latin America: Historical Studies of Chile and Brazil. New York 1969.

Galdames, L. et. al. Historiografía chilena. Santiago de Chile 1949.

Halperin, E. Nationalism and Communism in Chile. Cambridge, Mass. 1965.

Jobet, J. C. Ensayo crítico del desarrollo económico-social de Chile. Santiago de Chile 1955.

Moreno, F. J. Legitimacy and Stability in Latin America: A Study of Chilean Political Culture. New York 1969.

Nunn, F. M. Chilean Politics, 1920–1931: The Honorable Mission of the Armed Forces. Albuquerque 1970.

Olavaría Bravo, A. Chile bajo la Democracia Cristiana, 3 vols. Santiago de Chile 1966–67.

Petras, J. Politics and Social Forces in Chilean Development. Berkeley/Los Angeles 1969.

Solberg, C. E. Immigration and Nationalism: Argentina and Chile, 1890–1914. Austin 1970.

Universidad de Chile. Desarrollo de Chile en la primera mitad del siglo XX, 2 vols. Santiago de Chile 1953.

PERU

Astiz, C. A. Pressure Groups and Power Elites in Peruvian Politics. Ithaca 1969.

Basadre, J. Historia de la República del Perú, 10 vols. Lima 1961–64 (5th rev. edn).

Belaúnde, V. A. Peruanidad. Lima 1957 (2nd rev. edn).

Bourricaud, F. Power and Society in Contemporary Peru. New York 1970.

Caravedo, B. et. al. Estudios de psiquiatría social en el Perú. Lima 1963.

Chaplin, D. The Peruvian Industrial Labor Force. Princeton 1967.

Dobyns, H. F. The Social Matrix of Peruvian Indigenous Communities. Ithaca 1964.

Hilliker, G. G. The Politics of Reform in Peru: The Aprista and Other Mass Parties of Latin America. Baltimore 1970.

Matos Mar, J. et. al. El Perú actual: sociedad política. México 1970.

Pareja Paz Soldán, J. (ed.) Visión del Perú en el siglo XX, 2 vols. Lima 1962.

Payne, J. L. Labor and Politics in Peru: The System of Political Bargains. New Haven 1965.

Pike, F. B. The Modern History of Peru. London/New York 1967.

Sharp, D. A. (ed.) U.S. Foreign Policy in Peru. Austin 1972.

Stephens, R.H. *Wealth and Power in Peru.* Metuchen 1971.
Tauro, A. *Historia e historiadores del Perú.* Lima 1957.

ARGENTINA

Academia Nacional de Historia. *Historia de las presidencias.* Vols. I and II of *Historia argentina contemporánea.* Buenos Aires 1965.
Arrieta, R.A. (ed.) *Historia de la literature argentina,* 2 vols. Buenos Aires 1958–59.
Baily, S.L. *Labor, Nationalism and Politics in Argentina.* New Brunswick 1967.
Barager, J.R. (ed.) *Why Perón Came to Power: The Background to Peronismo in Argentina.* New York 1968.
Cúneo, D. *Compartamiento y crisis de la clase empresaria.* Buenos Aires 1967 (2nd edn).
Díaz Alejandro, C.E. *Essays on the Economic History of the Argentine Republic.* New Haven 1970.
Di Tella, T. *El sistema política argentino y la clase obrera.* Buenos Aires 1964.
Ferns, H.S. *Argentina.* New York 1969.
Germani, G. *Estructura social en la Argentina.* Buenos Aires 1955.
Goldwert, M. *Democracy, Militarism, and Nationalism in Argentina, 1930–1966.* Austin 1971.
Imaz, J.L. *Los que mandan.* Trans. into English by C.A. Astiz. Albany 1970.
Kennedy, J.J. *Catholicism, Nationalism, and Democracy in Argentina.* Notre Dame 1958.
Mafud, J. *Psicología de la viveza criolla: contribución para una interpretación de la realidad social argentina y americana.* Buenos Aires 1965.
Martínez Estrada, E. *X-Ray of the Pampa.* Trans. by A. Swietlicki. Austin 1971.
Potash, R.A. *The Army and Politics in Argentina, 1928–1945.* Stanford 1969.
Romero, J.L. *A History of Argentine Political Thought.* Trans. by T.F. McGann. Stanford 1963.
Scobie, J.R. *Argentina: A City and a Nation.* New York 1971 (2nd rev. edn).
Smith, P.H. *Politics and Beef in Argentina: Patterns of Conflict and Change.* New York 1969.
Snow, P. *Argentine Radicalism: The History and the Doctrines of the Radical Civic Union.* Iowa City 1965.
Walter, R.J. *Student Politics in Argentina: The University Reform and Its Effects, 1918–1964.* New York 1968.
Whitaker, A.P. *Argentina.* Englewood Cliffs 1964.

COLOMBIA

Cadavid, J.I. *Los fueros de la Iglesia ante el liberalismo y el conservatismo en Colombia: evolución político-religiosa de nuestros dos partidos, 1837–1955.* Medellín 1955.
Dix, R.H. *Colombia: The Political Dimensions of Change.* New Haven 1967.
Fals Borda, O. *Subversion and Social Change in Colombia.* New York 1969.
Fluharty, V.L. *Dance of the Millions: Military Rule and the Social Revolution in Colombia, 1930–1956.* Pittsburgh 1957.
Guzmán Campos, G. et al. *La violencia en Colombia: estudio de un proceso social,* 2 vols. Bogotá 1962.
Haddox, B.E. *Sociedad y religión en Colombia.* Trans. by J. Zalamea. Bogotá 1965.
Hagen, E.E. *El cambio social en Colombia: el factor humano en el desarrollo económico.* Bogotá 1963.
Jaramillo Uribe, J. *El pensamiento colombiano en el siglo XX.* Bogotá 1964.
Liévano Aguirre, I. *Los grandes conflictos sociales y económicos de nuestra historia.* Bogotá 1966 (2nd edn).
McGreevey, W.P. *An Economic History of Colombia, 1845–1930.* Cambridge, Eng. 1971.
Ospina Vázquez, L. *Industria y protección en Colombia, 1810–1930.* Medellín 1954.
Payne, J.L. *Patterns of Conflict in Colombia.* New Haven 1968.
Smith, T.L. *Colombia: Social Structure and the Process of Development.* Gainesville 1967–.
Urrutia, M. *The Development of the Colombian Labor Movement.* New Haven 1969.

CUBA

Aguilar, L.E. *Cuba 1933: Prologue to Revolution.* Ithaca 1972.
Barnett, C.R. and MacGaffey, W. *Cuba, Its People, Its Society, Its Culture.* New Haven 1962.
Bernardo, R.M. *The Theory of Moral Incentives in Cuba.* Tuscaloosa 1971.
Dewart, L. *Christianity and Revolution: The Lesson of Cuba.* New York 1963.
Draper, T. *Castroism: Theory and Practice.* New York 1965.
Dumont, R. *Cuba: Est-Il Socialiste?* Paris 1970.
Fagen, R.R. *The Transformation of Political Culture in Cuba.* Stanford 1969.
Guerra y Sánchez, R. *Sugar and Society in the Caribbean: An Economic History of Cuban Agriculture.* New Haven 1964.
Lockwood, L. *Castro's Cuba, Cuba's Fidel.* New York 1969.
Nelson, L. *Rural Cuba.* Minneapolis 1950.
O'Connor, J. *The Origins of Socialism in Cuba.* Ithaca 1970.
Roig de Leuchsenring, E. *Males y vicios de Cuba republicana.* Habana 1959.
Silverman, B. (ed.) *Man and Socialism in Cuba: The Great Debate.* New York 1972.
Smith, R.F. (ed.) *Background to Revolution: The Development of Modern Cuba.* New York 1966.
Suchlicki, J. *University Students and Revolution in Cuba, 1920–1968.* Coral Gables 1969.
Williams, W.A. *The United States, Cuba, and Castro.* New York 1962.

List of Illustrations

38 Allende supporters in a shanty town, 1964. Photo: Camera Press (Lynn Pelham).
39 President Salvador Allende with Fidel Castro in Santiago de Chile, November 1971. Photo: Camera Press (Diego Goldberg).
40 Map of Central and South America. Drawn by Claus Henning.
41 José Carlos Mariátegui; woodcut by José M. Valega.
42 Indians outside the church at Cajamarca, Peru. Photo: Picturepoint.
43 Víctor Raúl Haya de la Torre, 1969. Photo: Camera Press.
44 President Luis M. Sánchez Cerro (1889–1933). Photo: United Press International.
45 Railway in the province of Mendoza, Argentina, c. 1890. Photo: Radio Times Hulton Picture Library.
46 Harvesting scene in Argentina at the end of the nineteenth century; photograph by Dr Francisco Ayerzo. Academia Nacional de Bellas Artes, Buenos Aires.
47 De nuestro Cine: Mala Gente; Peronist poster by Arístides Rechaín, quoting Perón's words: 'A man who lives yet does not work is a despicable parasite preying on the efforts of those who do work.' Kunstgewerbemuseum, Zürich.
48 Juan Perón (b. 1895) at the theatre in Buenos Aires with his wife, Eva. Photo: Mas.
49 Eva Perón (1919–52) visiting a children's home. Photo: Mas.
50 The Presidential Family; painting by Fernando Botero, 1967. Collection Museum of Modern Art, New York. Gift of Mr and Mrs Warren D. Benedeck.
51 Jorge Eliécer Gaitán (1902–48). Photo: United Press International.
52 Gaitán's body surrounded by university students, 21 April 1948. Photo: United Press International.
53 President John F. Kennedy lays a brick during the dedication of a low-rent housing project in Colombia sponsored by the Alliance for Progress. Photo: USIA.
54 The Farm; painting by Rafael Moreno, 1943. Collection Museum of Modern Art, New York. Inter-American Fund.
55 Cuban poster commemorating the Day of the Heroic Guerrilla; published by the Organization of Solidarity with Asia, Africa and Latin America (OSPAAL).
56 Fidel Castro with Nikita Khrushchev in the Soviet Union, 1964. Photo: Camera Press.
57 Fidel Castro in the sugar fields, 1972. Photo: Camera Press.
58 Poor families from Lima occupying land in the Pamplona district. Photo: Camera Press (Prensa Latina).
59 Peruvian troops parading before the monument to Colonel Francisco Bolognesi Cervantes, patron of the Peruvian army, watched by Church dignitaries. Photo: Camera Press (Prensa Latina).

Index

Page numbers in italics refer to illustrations

Encina, Francisco Antonio 16
England 31, 36
Ernst, Adolfo 75
Estado social del Perú durante la dominación española
(Prado y Ugarteche) 16
estancieros 85
Estenssoro, Víctor Paz *see* Paz Estenssoro, Víctor
Europe 26

Falange, the 99
Falcoff, Mark 122
fascism 139
Federal War 73, 75
Ferreria, J. Alfredo 18
First World War 36, 39, 94, 132
fisheries 164
foreign investment in Spanish American
countries 39–40, 140–1, 157
Fortoul, Gil *see* Gil Fortoul, José
France 66
Franco, Francisco 99
Frei Montalva, Eduardo *100*, 101
Fromm, Erich 26

Gaitán, Jorge Eliécer 133–4, *135*, 136, 137
Gall, Norman 157
Gallegos, Rómulo 79
Gálvez, Manuel 118–19, 145
gañanes 93
García Calderón, Francisco 129
García Cubas, Antonio 15
gauchos 71
Generation of 1910 131
Gil Fortoul, José 19
Glazer, Myron 145
Gómez, Juan Vicente 23, 76–81
Gómez, Laureano 133–4, 136
González Prada, Manuel 107–8, 159
Grace Contract 106
Grau San Martín, Ramón 147
Great Britain 110
Grupo de Izquierda 60
Grupo de la Democracia Cristiana 100–1
Grupo Túpac Amaru 60
guano supply 106
Guatemala 10
Guevara, 'Che' 66, 152, *153*, 158
Guzmán Blanco, Antonio 73–5, 77, 105

Hamuy, Eduardo 98
Havana 156
Haya de la Torre, Víctor Raúl 111, *112*, 114
Herrera, Luis Alberto de 24
Hispanic American Historical Review 15
Hispanic culture 36–7
Hocschilds, the 59, 68

Ibañez del Campo, Colonel Carlos; and economic reform 95, 97, 105, 125, 132; and presidency 98; and seizure of power 93, 95
Ideal de la humanidad para la vida (Krause) 19
illiteracy *see* education
immigration 117–18, 152

Inca civilization 108–9
Indians; South American: alleged inferiority of
15–16, 57, 98; glorification of 50, 107;
reformation of 16, 29, 43, 58, 68, 107, 151,
159–60; self-sufficiency of 10; *see also* Aymara
Indians; Quechua Indians
indigenistas 59, 108–9
inflation 30–1, 47, 63
Ingenieros, José 15
inquilinos 94
Inquisition 78
International Petroleum Company 110, 165
Iquique 94

Jiménez, Major Marcos Pérez *see* Pérez Jiménez,
Major Marcos
justicialismo 123, 126

Karol, K. S. 152
Kennedy, President John F. 140
Korean War 115
Krause, Karl Christian Friedrich 19–20, 25, 89
Krausism 44, 119

labour unions 31, 36, 47, 69, 95
La Brea Parinas oilfields 111
La Escuela Positiva 18
Lamas, Carlos Saavedra *see* Saavedra Lamas,
Carlos
Lanz, Laureano Vallenilla *see* Vallenilla Lanz,
Laureano
La Prensa 160
Las profesiones liberales en el Perú (Villarán) 107
Laureanistas 133–4
Leguía, Augusto B. 110–11, 113–14, 121, 132
Leo XIII, Pope 23
Leoni, Raúl 79, 82
Letelier, Valentín 19
Lewis, Oscar 53
liberalism 19, 25, 50, 118, 120
Lieuwen, Edwin 80
Lima 106–7, 159
llaneros 71–2
López Contreras, Eleazar 79
López Pumarejo, Alfonso 135
Luco, Ramón Barros *see* Barros Luco, Ramón
Lugones, Leopoldo 118

Machado, Gerardo 147, 149
Mac-Iver, Enrique 19
Madero, Francisco I. 44, *49*
Maeztu, Ramiro de 36
Magnet, Alejandro 125
Mao Tse-tung 152
Mariátegui, José Carlos 108–10, 151, 159
Marof, Tristán *see* Navarro, Gustavo Adolfo
Martínez, Martín C. 86, 88
Marx, Karl 26
Marxism: Bolivian 64; Cuban 154, 157; Mexican
44; South American 144, 150, 164
Marxists: Bolivian 60; Chilean 97; Colombian
134; Mexican 51; Peruvian 110, 164; Spanish
American 146

railways 106, 126
Razón y Fe 23
'Rebel Army', Cuban 157
Recabarren, Luis Emilio 18
René-Moreno, Gabriel 58
Revista de las Españas (Maeztu) 36
Revolution *see* Mexican Revolution of 1910
Reyes, Rafael 131
Ricardo, David 130
Riva Agüero, José de la 24
Rodó, José Enrique 21, 44, 89
Rojas Pinilla, Gustavo 137 ·
Rojas Pinilla de Moreno, María Eugenia 137
rosca 59, 64
Ross Santa María, Gustavo 96, 114
Russia 31, 154
Russians, the 152
Ruta cultural del Perú (Valcárcel) 107

Saavedra, Bautista 59, 65
Saavedra Lamas, Carlos 123
Saenz Peña, Roque 121
Sánchez, Ramón Díaz *see* Díaz Sánchez, Ramón
Sánchez Cerro, Luis M. 113, 14
San Martín, Ramón Grau *see* Grau San Martín, Ramón
Santa Marta 133
Santiago 94, 102
Santiago de Cuba 149
Scalabrini Ortiz, Raúl 122
Sebreli, Juan José 127
Second World War: and national economies 97, 114, 139; and politics 99; and social conditions 99, 135, 138, 142, 144, 168
secularism 25, 27, 146
sesenta, the 75
Sierra, Justo 43
silver resources 106
sinarquista movement 24
sindicatos 67
Smith, Adam 97, 130
Socarrás, Carlos Prío *see* Prío Socarrás, Carlos
Sociología de Lima (Capelo) 106
Soler, Mariano (later Archbishop of Montevideo) 88
Spain: and Jews 152; and lower classes 65, 71, 86, 89; and politics 100, 157; and social values 11, 86; and upper classes 89
Spencer, Herbert 15, 97
Standard Oil Company 76, 111
sub-culture: amalgamation with dominant culture 83, 110, 151; anthropology of 71–2; asserted inferiority of 15–16, 43, 57, 59, 76, 148; asserted superiority of 59, 68, 107; attitude towards dominant culture 83, 110, 151; and Catholic Church 24, 26, 46, 86, 110, 124, 132, 143; discontent of 29, 94, 98, 110, 130, 135–6, 148, 162; economic condition of 9–10, 30–1, 38, 48, 57, 63, 65–6, 70, 83, 87, 93, 107, 124, 130, 148, 149, 159, 161; and education 20, 35, 73, 75, 77; influence on dominant

culture 44, 107, 110; materialism of 119–20, 124, 146; and politics 46, 72–3, 87, 102–3, 119, 121, 124, 133, 149; population movements of 93, 122, 130; reform of 12, 16–17, 19–20, 25–7, 43–4, 48–52, 57, 63, 65, 67–8, 72, 76, 83, 107, 110–12, 119, 123–4, 136, 141–4, 160, 167–8; resignation of 10, 105, 132, 134; values of 11–12, 19–20, 28, 30, 44, 53, 65, 67, 87, 89, 108, 142, 146, 168
sugar industry 132, 148, 155, 156
Switzerland 86

Táchira 75–6, 79
Tamayo, Franz 60
Tarma 114
taxation 86, 88, 90, 111, 115
Terry, Fernando Belaúnde *see* Belaúnde Terry, Fernando
textile industry 132
Thomas, Hugh 147
tin production 67, 68–9
Tirano Banderas (Valle-Inclán) 38
Toro, David 64
Tse-tung, Mao *see* Mao Tse-tung
tupamaros 90, 91

Unamuno, Miguel de 118
Unión Cívica Radical *see* Argentinian Radical Party
United Fruit Company 132–3
United States: attitudes towards 21–2, 44, 55; economic conditions of 31; and immigration of Cubans 152; involvement in economies of Spanish American countries 16, 38–40, 69, 95, 101, 110–11, 126, 137, 140–1, 148, 152–3, 164; as model 133, 139, 143–4, 151; and politics of Spanish American countries 9, 147
United States Business Investments in Foreign Countries (United States Department of Commerce) 39
universities *see* education, higher
University Reform movement 34–5, 121
upper classes *see* dominant culture
Uruguay: and Catholic Church 24; and demography 85, 141; and dominant culture 85–7, 90; and economics 29, 86–7, 89–90; and education 89; and politics 85–7, *88*; and social amenities 89, 132; and social structure 70, *84*, 85, 88–9, 91, 158; and sub-culture 29, 85–7, 90

Valcárcel, Luis E. 107
Valle-Inclán, Ramón 38
Vallenilla Lanz, Laureano 19, 76
Valparaíso 94
Varela, Pedro José 89
Vatican, the 23, 115, 133
Vatican Council, Second 144–5
Velasco Alvarado, General Juan 162
Véliz, Claudio 36
vendepatrias 68, 122

Venezuela: and Catholic Church 23, 74; and dominant culture 82, 146, 150, 157; and economics 82–3, 142; and paternalism 19; and politics 81, 105, 132; and Protestantism 74; and social structure 71, 91, 157, 168; and sub-culture 83, 105; and United States investment 40

Verba, Sidney 52
Villa, Pancho 17
Villarán, Manuel Vicente 106–7
Villarroel, Gualberto 64–5
Villavicencio, Rafael 75

War of the Pacific 56, 57, 59, 105, 107
welfare, social 97, 115, 143, 148, 156
Wilkie, Professor James W. 69

yanaconas 159
Yankees 21–2
Yrigoyen, Hipólito 119–20

Zapata, Emiliano 17, *45*
Zea, Leopoldo 46